THE GIFFORDS OF EXETER

The English Branch of an Irish Family

Nancy O'Connell Ronning, MLS, MS

Copyright © 2020 Nancy Ronning
All rights reserved.
978-0-9838375-2-7

The front cover illustration is the Crest of the City of Exeter granted in 1564.

The map on the back cover is a photograph of an 1804 J. Roper engraving. It is in the collection of the author.

DEDICATION

For Yvonne Hensman, a brilliant researcher who was my tour guide on the streets of Exeter, my docent at the Non-Conformist Cemetery, my dear friend, and transatlantic companion.

And to my children and grandchildren so that they might know and be proud of their English heritage – not just names and dates, but lives.

"there is an old proverb that says, 'We die once when the last breath leaves our bodies. We die a second time when the last person speaks our name.' The first death is beyond our control. But the second one we can strive to prevent."

The Book of Lost Friends by Lisa Wingate 2019

CONTENTS

Dedication iii
Acknowledgments ix
1   England 1
     1649 – 1820
2   Trade 4
3   Exeter 8
4   Apprenticeship 13
5   Religion 15
6   The Family 19
7   John Gifford 21
     c1630 – 1688
8   Thomas Gifford 24
     c1616 – 1688
9   William Gifford 26
     1700 – 1757
10 Honour Hutchings Gifford 30
     – 1759
11 William Gifford 32
     1728 – 1787/8
12 Martha Whitelock 36
     1743 – 1798
13 William & Martha's Children
     Henry, Matilda, Charlotte, Samuel 38
14 Charlotte Gifford 41
     c1775 – 1849
15 Anne Kelly 45
     c1820 – c1858
16 The Peerage 47
Epilogue 53

THE GIFFORDS OF EXETER

APPENDICES

WILLS OF:

I	John Gifford 1688	55
II	Thomas Gifford 1718	56
III	Ann Norrish Gifford 2 February 1758	59
IV	William Gifford 1753	63
V	Honour Hutchings Gifford 1760	69
VI	William Gifford 1788	73
VII	Martha Whitelock 1798	77
VIII	Charlotte Gifford 1849	81

About the Author 91

ACKNOWLEDGMENTS

The members of the Devon Family History Society who sent me the register of Gifford burials in the Non-Conformist Cemetery in Exeter that set me on the road to discovery.

Robert Dymond, author of *"History of the Suburban Parish of St. Leonard, Exeter"* the booklet that gave me the 1794 marriage record of the Irish Lt. Lewis Kelly to Miss Charlotte Gifford of St. Leonard's Parish, Exeter, enabling me to begin this English journey.

It is through their amazing wills which are available online from the National Archives of Britain that we know so much about the Giffords. It is the challenge of the script that compelled me to include the transcriptions in an appendix.

Yvonne Hensman has been generous in sharing her transcriptions. But since my copy of Microsoft Word does not talk to hers, I have retyped her work, and included it with a note to that effect. My typing is notoriously bad, any and all errors are mine alone.

THE GIFFORDS OF EXETER

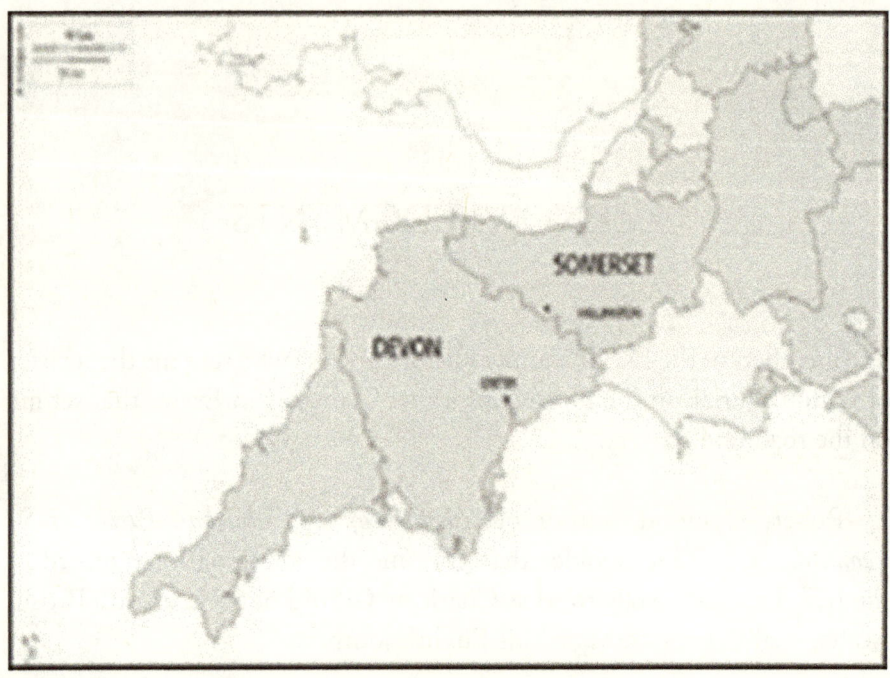

The South of England

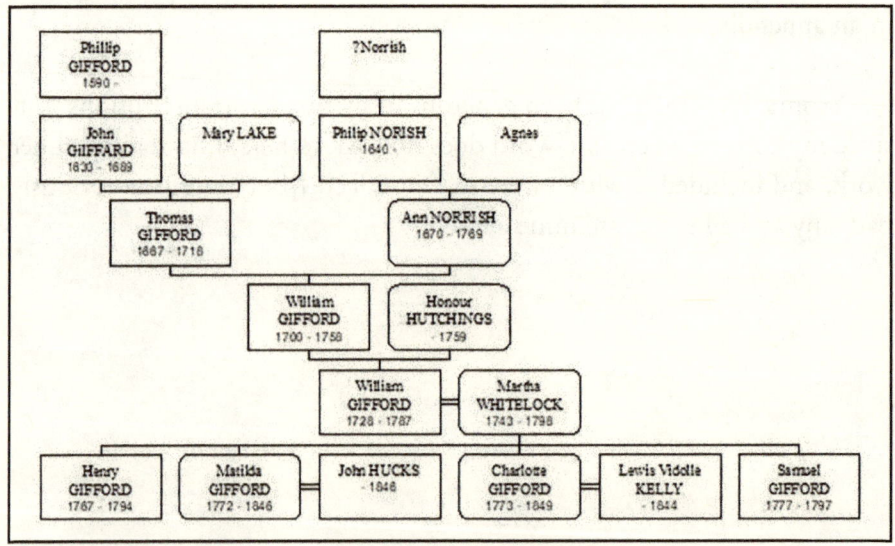

The Giffords of Exeter

1
ENGLAND
1649 – 1820

Our Gifford family roots lie deep in the soil of Wellington, Somerset and Exeter, Devon in the southwest of England. Our earliest probable ancestor was born in the late 1500s, the earliest documented was certainly Thomas who was born in 1667 and married Ann Norrish in 1682. Their son, William was apprenticed to a Grocer in Exeter in 1711, and moved our branch of the family there.

In order to tell the story of that family it is necessary to look at the social, religious, economic and political history of the country and of the towns in which they lived.

Between 1603 and 1820 our ancestors lived in a volatile England ruled by ten different monarchs, each of whom turned their different religious, social and personal preferences into law. James I ruled from 1609 – 1625 during which time he suppressed the Catholic and Puritan religions. It was during his reign, in 1620, that the Pilgrims of Mayflower fame left from Plymouth in Devon for America to escape persecution.

After James, Charles I was king from 1625 to 1649. He was a high Anglican with an Italian Catholic princess wife, and believed that he alone should rule according to God's plan. He therefore dissolved Parliament three times, incurring the wrath of its members. Parliament reacted and England endured a nine year period of Civil Wars from 1642 – 1651 during which the Parliamentary parties tried to take control of the government out of the King's hands.

But Charles I strongly believed in the Divine Right of Kings and would not compromise with the Parliamentarians who then captured him, and removed him from the throne. He escaped, was recaptured, tried for treason and was beheaded in 1649. The monarchy was dissolved.

Then fanatically Puritan Oliver Cromwell cruelly ruled the "Commonwealth" as Lord Protector of England, Scotland and Ireland until he died and was buried in Westminster Cathedral in 1658. (His body was later dug up and reburied elsewhere.) His exploits in Ireland make his name anathema to this day. His son Richard Cromwell succeeded him, ruled ineptly, and resigned two years later in 1660.

Parliament then invited Charles II, the exiled son of Charles I, to return from his exile in Catholic France, and gave him the throne by an Act of Parliament. He was neither Catholic enough or Protestant enough for any faction. He died without an heir in 1685.

Charles' brother, next in the line of succession, ruled as James II from 1685 until 1688. He was a convert to Catholicism but raised his two daughters as Protestants. The State religion was again something of a puzzle. When he died three years later without a male heir, leaving the throne empty, William of Orange in the Netherlands successfully invaded England in what was called the Glorious Revolution.

Because he and his Protestant wife Mary were both grandchildren of Charles I, they had some claim to the throne and so were invited by Parliament to become the King and Queen of England, Scotland and Ireland. Both were staunch Protestants. Mary died in 1694, but William continued to reign until 1702.

Their reign marked the end of any tolerance for Catholics or Non-Conformists and the ascent of the Dutch Protestant religion. Again the monarchs were childless. They were succeeded by Anne, Mary's sister (also by Act of Parliament). She died in 1707 and was followed by Queen Anne, the daughter of James II who ruled until 1714, at which time George I of Hanover became King because he was her closest Protestant relation. Catholics were now forbidden from occupying the throne of England.

And so, for one hundred eleven years the throne was occupied by ten different rulers, whose beliefs differed widely in politics, religion, and world view. With each change in religion the members of the "out" religion were persecuted. Although it was a period of instability, trade flourished, probably because England was so busy with its internal problems that it had no time or funds for warfare against neighbors who were the trading partners of its people . . . and our people, the Giffords, now of Exeter.

If this foray into British history is mind-numbing in its complexity, it is difficult to imagine what life was like under the shifting demands of kings and queens who each ruled by Divine Right. Stability was a concept imagined – only imagined.

2
TRADE

Since medieval times in England, professions and trades were rigidly organized. One did not decide to " become" a lawyer or a blacksmith or a linen draper. There were trade associations in each city with strict rules governing just about everything in each profession and in the lives of those who practiced the profession. These societies were called Guilds. Such systems were to be found in ancient Greece, Egypt and the East, and there was a guild in Exeter in the year 1000. The English guilds as we know them began in the Middle Ages. In those religious times, each had a patron saint.

Other than pictures of the historic building on the High Street, I have not been able to find anything specific to the Linen Draper's Guild of Exeter, but a glance at its London counterpart will be fascinating and instructive.

"The Worshipful Company of Drapers" is one of the original 110 livery companies, and also one of the "Great Twelve," the most influential of all the guilds of the City of London. Its full name is "Wardens and Brethren and Sisters of the Guild or Fraternity of the Blessed Mary the Virgin of the Mystery of Drapers of the City of London," often simply as the Drapers Company. The beautiful, medieval Drapers' Crest and motto "Unto God Only be Honor and Glory" would have been displayed at each member's shop and in the GuildHall over the member's chair.

Since I was unable to decode their beautiful crest, I sent an email to the present day Guild in London, and overnight received the following reply from their archivist.

THE GIFFORDS OF EXETER

Dear Ms Ronning

Thank you for your enquiry concerning the Company's coat of arms. Guilds once existed throughout England, controlling and regulating the trades in their respective towns and cities, as well as overseeing the training of those learning their trades, looking after the interests and welfare of those working and extending their social concern to their neighbours and others further afield. They were, therefore, by their very nature, independent of each other.

However, many of the guilds, and trades, used the coat of arms of the London guilds the imagery becoming a recognised symbol for a trade.

The motto has always been in English; the ram symbolizes both the wool trade (a 'golden' and profitable trade which the Company once regulated) and is a common symbol for prosperity; the device on the shield symbolizes the Company's patron saint, the Blessed Virgin Mary.

Please do not hesitate to contact me should you have any further queries.

Yours sincerely,
Penny

The imposing Exeter GuildHall continues its 600 years as the site of local government. It clearly boasts its centrality to life in the town, and to the affluence and influence of its members. The original medieval building has been on this site since the fourteenth century and its medieval origins are apparent to visitors. The front was added in 1500, and the elaborate columns in 1594. The interior was modernized in the eighteenth century. Our Gifford ancestor members must have gone here regularly, and enjoyed the prestige that arose from belonging.

As I walked beneath the columns, I could almost feel their pride in this remarkable place. If the exterior is grand, its interior is spectacular. It has a cathedral like feeling, with stained glass window and stalls, like choir stalls, each bearing the crest of one of the guilds. "Our" Linen Drapers crest is on the right, close to where I was standing when I took this photograph.

The Linen Drapers Medieval Guild of Exeter, like all other guilds, regulated both the number of members admitted to a trade as well as the rules by which they did business. By doing so they kept prices high and stable, and eliminated job-switching for their apprentices. No member ever lowered a price or had a sale. No apprentice found a 'job' with better working conditions or a shorter apprenticeship. Competition was not permitted, and the masters ruled the trade in every aspect. Should anyone break the rules they were expelled from the guild and therefore unable to practice their trade or craft. It almost never happened.

The Drapers Guild was rich in ceremony and in public manifestations of its importance. In addition to its crest, a guild had tokens, ceremonial dress for its officers, elaborate coffin covers for the funerals of those officers, and other more practical items such as advertising cards called "trade cards." Crests were located above their shops and on ceremonial papers and linens, and tokens were used for advertising.

This beautiful trade card of an Irish Linen Draper in London exemplifies the wealth and the geographical scope the trade. A linen draper would have a very significant commitment of money in the shop itself, in the merchandise in the shop, and in the ships and cargo navigating the treacherous English Channel carrying their goods to ports in Flanders and beyond. It was a highly desirable trade which was only open to the sons of prosperous families who could afford the high apprenticeship fee .

The customers of the Draper were ladies and gentlemen as shown in this trade card that depicts the elegance of a similar draper's shop in Bristol where ladies and gentlemen would go to order their new clothing. Considering that ladies of the period changed dresses at least twice, if not three times a day, the drapers were busy, and prosperous.

William Gifford added wine from Portugal to his ship's cargo and business boomed. The English fondness for Port also contributed to its use as ballast for the ships returning from Portugal. Life must have been much more pleasant for the merchants of Exeter, and for our Gifford family as their trade increased and their Non-Conformist friends also did well and became more prominent in Exeter society.

3
EXETER

The Exeter of our ancestors had a crowded business center, suburbs, and large country estates which in that way resemble modern cities and their environs. It boasts a Roman wall, and a town center dominated by the huge and glorious gothic Exeter Cathedral. The first church was founded in 1050, but construction on the present site began in 1114. Two Norman towers survive. There was a major rebuilding between 1270 and 1350. It is surrounded by a 'close,' much lawn and a series of buildings that once served the cathedral, but now are shops, homes, restaurants and the recently burned Royal Clarence Hotel.

In 1700 Exeter was a very busy city, second only to London in the number of ships that sailed up its river, the Exe. Unlike little towns in the previous century where farming was the way of life for ninety percent of the population, Exeter's wealth came mainly from new industry and international trade. Woolen goods were exported to Germany, Flanders, Holland, Spain, Portugal, and the islands in the Mediterranean; linen was brought back as ballast in the ships from Germany and Flanders, and wine arrived from the Mediterranean and Portugal.

The social structure of Exeter reflected this new division within the society. Its population of about 11,200 people existed in three distinct classes among which there was little or no contact other than business. The upper class were the people who had homes around the Cathedral Close and the quarter between the South and East Gates of the city. These families would also have had large estates in the countryside and used their town houses for the "season." On an average their annual incomes were about £300 – £400. The value of their homes was gauged by the number of hearths (fireplaces) with the wealthiest having ten or more and the poorest having only one.

THE GIFFORDS OF EXETER

Shops selling food, footwear, and the linen drapers establishments were situated along the Main Street. Thomas Gifford owned one of those shops. The building still exists.

One ever present danger in Exeter, as well as other crowded cities and towns, was the constant threat of fire. As early as 1626 Exeter "employed a machine designed for putting out fires. The crude and heavy pumping engine was kept in the GuildHall from where it was carried to the fire." But when the too occasional fires broke out in thatch, kitchens or chimneys, locals attacked it with pots of water, and tore fiery thatch from rooves to stop the fire from spreading. Often to no avail.

Groups of private citizens formed small, local companies, and employed private fire brigades who would be called out to deal with fires in their customers' homes or establishments. One of these, the West of England Fire and Life Insurance Company, began in 1808 after a fire destroyed two-thirds of the houses in a neighboring town. An article in the *Cumberland Pacquet* of Tuesday, October 7, 1828 names Board members Henry Francis Brooke, Esq. President, Wearman Gifford, Esq. (our many times great uncle) and T. Edmund Granger as Vice presidents.

Prominently attached to the home of each of the West of England's insureds was a lead emblem, often bearing the policy holder's identification number, and which signaled to the fire brigade that they were to respond to fires in this establishment. One of these plaques, by some strange fate, is housed at the American History Museum, a part of the Smithsonian Institution. There were other fire companies as well, and each responded to its own customers. City life was not easy.

The education of its children is surely a measure of the wealth, sophistication and values of a city. Fortunately, the *Besley's Exeter Directory, for 1835*, in a section entitled 'Public Institutions for Education,' lists 17 schools, and includes address, date of founding, mission, number of pupils (boys and girls) and the Presidents or Patrons. I found them fascinating reading, and was pleased to learn that Wearman Gifford was President of a school. Because of their differences from Twenty-first Century life, three things stand out. First, knitting was part of the curriculum for girls, not a hobby, but a life skill. Ladies did needlework, and patronized linen drapers and seamstresses. Common people knitted. Second, boys and girls finished school at fourteen years old, and went to work – either to an apprenticeship or to service. Third, Exeter had daycare in 1825. Amazing!

Following are excerpts from just five of the seventeen schools:

BLUE MAID's SCHOOL Mary Arches Street. Founded in 1671. In this establishment four girls are maintained, clothed, and instructed in reading, sewing and knitting. – They are admitted between the ages of seven and ten and discharged at fourteen years old, when they are bound apprentices with a premium of four pounds each, or placed as servants in respectable families. *Trustees,* The Right Worshipful Mayor and Chamber. – *Mistress* Jane Dicker

EPISCOPAL CHARITY SCHOOLS, Paul Street, open to the children of all Exeter parishes. Established in 1708. By this Benevolent establishment 180 boys and 130 girls are clothed and educated: boys in reading writing and arithmetic; the girls in reading, sewing and knitting. They are admitted at the age of seven and continue till twelve. The schools are supported by legacies, benefactions, subscriptions, and collections of the parish churches. *Perpetual Patron and President,* The Rt. Rev, the Lord Bishop.

LADIES SCHOOL, Holloway Street. This school was established by a society of ladies in 1804, for the improvement of the Female Poor in Exeter. The girls are clothed, and instructed in reading, the church catechism, plain sewing, knitting and marking. They are admitted at the age of seven and discharged at fourteen.

PROTESTANT DISSENTERS' CHARITY SCHOOL, Paris street. This school was instituted in 1710, and is supported by legacies, benefactions subscriptions and collections. There are at present in the school 33 boys and 24 girls who are clothed and instructed in reading, writing, and arithmetic; the girls are taught sewing and knitting. **President, Wearman Gifford** [emphasis mine]-Treasurer, Bar. P Pope – *School Master,* Jas. Bowden, *School Mistress,* Sarah Bowden.

DEVON AND EXETER INFANT SCHOOL, established September 1825, opened Feby 4 1828. Children are allowed to enter as soon as they can walk, and are taken care of from the hours of 9 in the morning until 5 in the afternoon. About 125 children attend school daily. *Patron* The Rt. Rev the Lord Bishop of Exeter- *President* The Right Honorable Lord Rolle- *Vice-President-* Viscount Ebrington MP etc.

The country homes, on the other hand, were large, set in rural places so that families could accommodate their friends and relatives for hunting and fishing parties and to escape the noise and filth of the poor, crowded town. Yvonne Hensman found one of these lovely homes and arranged for us to visit.

It hardly seems possible, but Foxdown Manor was once the property of John Hucks whose wife, Matilda, was a daughter of our Gifford family in Exeter. When I visited with Yvonne and Richard Hensman, a family not only lived in Foxdown, but ran an exclusive B&B in all its lovely rooms. It has since been sold, and is once again the family home of a young couple and their children.

It has a chicken coop which is possibly original, and integral to the story of the house's name. Foxes were very prevalent in the area, and it was the rare chicken that survived to make a really good dinner. So the coop was designed sturdily enough to foil the predators. It is difficult to describe the remoteness of the house. But as we approached it, my friend Richard Hensman's car totally filled the space between two rows of hedges on what was called a "country lane," the only access road.

The other sections of Exeter were densely built and inhabited by the less prosperous citizens. Waste was thrown out windows, sewage ran in the streets, and life was hard. The Giffords lived in Saint Olav's Parish and Saint Petrocks Parish of Exeter. The houses were described and taxed and the wealth of the inhabitants was displayed to all who could  count the number of visible chimneys in each home. The poorest 1,073 families lived in hovels with only one hearth, two thirds of the Exeter families had between three and six hearths and one third had six to ten hearths. 62 families had ten or more. The gap between the rich and the poor was dramatic.

Many of our ancestors lived in St. Leonard's Parish, in the days when it was outside the walls of Exeter , just "beyond the grasp of the municipal tax collector." An early paper boasts that it had " neither lawyer, nor parson, nor doctor, nor pauper, nor poor-rate, nor pound, nor barrack, nor soldier, nor tavern, nor ale-house nor anything that could be called a nuisance," *Exeter Sixty Years Ago*, by Sir John Bowring, LLD 1805. The 1801 English census reports its entire population to be 133 people in 26 houses, and those numbers had probably been nearly the same for centuries.

But when the first William came to Exeter in 1711, he came as an apprentice to a grocer named Anthony Vicary. A grocer of the 1700's was not as high on the social scale as a line draper, but he was still a man of means who produced some of his goods himself, but often purchased the rest from local farmers or occasionally from farther away. Grocers were town folk and respected for their merchandizing skills. They also advertised with "trade cards," the illustrated business card of the day.

This grocer's trade card lists an impressive array of products, domestic and imported. They are: "tea, coffee, chocolate, Best Spanish scotch, Portugale [sic] snuff, Blues and starch (for laundering) Rum, Coniac,[sic] Brandy, Batavia Arrack (thick, sweet molasses from Java) neat as imported (not watered down)."

One level up the ladder of retail success from grocer was the trade of the draper. Thomas' son William eventually became a Linen Draper, a category which was retail hierarchy. Drapers were purely middlemen whose skill in acquiring, evaluating, and merchandizing special lines of goods ranked them among the ranks of skilled tradesmen - specialists, whose fortunes were better than the many grocers who were found in every town. Silversmiths, goldsmiths and hops merchants were among the skilled tradesmen.

For the first time in history there was room for exceptional upward mobility via the wealth earned in trade, and sometimes via marriage between classes. Trade was just becoming marginally respectable.

It might be interesting to examine the apprentice system in England at the time, keeping in mind that William Gifford's apprenticeship which began in 1711 almost certainly lasted for seven years.

4
APPRENTICESHIP

English apprenticeship was the system, begun in medieval times, by which young English men (also some few women) learned a trade, so that the professions were assured of a suitable number of young practitioners. According to an Apprenticeship Law, passed in 1563, anyone who wished to enter a trade had to serve a seven-year apprenticeship. By 1601, in an effort to control the number of children of paupers and those "overburdened with children" the law was extended and apprenticeship was made mandatory for anyone under the age of 21. Refusal resulted in imprisonment until the child or man found a master. To ensure enough places for apprentices, any man who owned a piece of land that he could cultivate in one year with one ox-team was obliged to take on an apprentice.

By the eighteenth century apprenticeship existed at every level of society except the highest, those Esquires or nobles who relied on rents and family money rather than trade. Our Irish ancestor, Lewis Kelly, who married Charlotte Gifford is always given the title "Esq," signaling that he lived on his income.

Although apprenticeships were usually for seven years, a few, attorneys, dressmakers, milliners and doctors would serve for only five. The longest apprenticeships, fourteen years, were served by orphans, unwanted children, bastards and stepchildren. Their masters, the butchers, blacksmiths, shoemakers and chimney sweeps required long hours of drudgery.

"Many times small children would get stuck inside the twisted chimney which caused serious health complications and sometimes death. This practice of sending small boys up and down chimneys in order to ensure that they were free of harmful creosote deposits was the norm in England for approximately 200 years". (Google)

THE GIFFORDS OF EXETER

Today it seems inconceivable that a child of four or five years could be a chimney sweeper's apprentice until he was nineteen years old, if he survived. Most did not. Fortunately our ancestors were not chimneysweeps or their apprentices, but if they owned homes with multiple chimneys, they regularly employed the services of these men and their children apprentices.

The Sweep had to be paid for taking on the child, therefore the parents of the apprentice, the Parish, or the church paid the Master a set fee, and the child lived in the Master's home, and became, in effect, a working member of the family. Treatment varied widely.

Fortunately for our research, in the year 1710 Parliament passed the Stamp Tax which required a tax on each indenture document. Our ancestor, William Gifford was apprenticed in 1711. Following is a record of his indenture.

When William Gifford came to Exeter just one year after records began, the family of a grocer's apprentice paid between £30 to £40 to the Master, in this case Anthony Vicary, though no monetary figure is given on this transcription of William's apprenticeship papers. Anthony Vicary probably had other apprentices with overlapping terms so that he would always have a skilled helper as well as one or two in training.

According to Joan Lane's *Apprenticeship in England, 1600 to 1914*, Grocer apprentices had to "write a neat hand, count, be alert at weighing out, and give the Master the Advantage of the Scales." To become a Grocer required a large outlay of money, as stock had to be bought, premises acquired, and enough extra cash had to be available to cover bad debts. (p.105)

When, in 1742 William was himself a Master, he took on John Fryer as his apprentice and received a premium of £157,10s, an increase of £127 in just 29 years, for the seven year commitment. His papers say that John Fryer was Portuguese. But it is probable that he was probably a wine/port merchant working out of Oporto. There is a baptismal record for a John Fryer on 9 September 1721 at the Bow Meeting in Exeter. His mother is Elizabeth and his father John, a dyer. So William appears to have taken the son of a colleague and fellow religionist into his home as an apprentice.

It was not uncommon for a promising apprentice to marry the master's daughter, and John Fryer must have been a stellar apprentice for he did just that. He and Ann Gifford were married in 1752, just three years after the end of his seven year apprenticeship.

5
RELIGION

In addition to business, an overriding determinant of social status and lifestyle was religion. It is impossible to overemphasize the importance of the role of religion in the lives of English men and women at this time.

William and his parents were Non-Conformists in an England whose official religion had rocketed back and forth among Roman Catholic, Church of England and Puritan denominations. According to Wikipedia the term Non-Conformist referred generally to any Protestant Christian who did not "conform" to the governance and usages of the established Church of England.

The Act of Uniformity in 1662 required churchmen to use all rites and ceremonies as prescribed in the Book of Common Prayer, the Church of England book of rites. It also required Church of England ordination of all ministers. Consequently, because they refused ordination in that denomination, nearly 2,000 clergymen were "ejected" from the established Church for refusing to comply with the provisions of the Act.

Thereafter, a Non-Conformist was identified as any English subject belonging to a church other than the Church of England. In the mid 1600's Quakers started to move into Exeter. They were arrested and imprisoned if they were found, and all of their property was seized. Strict religious practices were enforced by law. Attendance at a Church of England Sunday service was mandatory under the law, and fines could be levied for non-attendance . In 1720 Exeter would not license traveling players within the city walls, so all theatre took place outside the walls. Life was to be simple, strict and filled with religion. Fun was not on the agenda.

Because religion was an overwhelming determiner of almost everything in the life of an Englishman at this time, and because many of the great merchants of Devon were Non-Conformists, they were excluded from public posts and societies. They therefore directed their considerable energy and attention to business and their guilds, thereby assuring their wealth.

Our ancestors belonged to an Exeter Non-Conformists chapel called the Bow Meeting. This "chapel" and other Non-Conformist chapel members socialized with one another and did business among themselves and also with the Protestant Germans and Dutch, as well as the Catholic Portuguese, Spanish and Italians. Because their wives and families were also excluded from orthodox schools and society, they formed their own tight-knit societies. Theirs was an intimate, busy circle. Families functioned, educated their children, worshiped, married, died and were buried within the framework of Non-Conformist friends and neighbors and with the ceremony and protection of the Guild.

EXETER DISSENTERS' GRAVEYARD

Among the privileges easily taken for granted by generations who never imagined the severe restrictions imposed on Non-Conformists, was the fact that cemeteries were owned by and reserved for practicing members of the Church of England. This left an entire community with no place to bury their dead. Exeter's Non-Conformists met this problem with decisive action. In 1748 members of the Bow Meeting and the Little Meeting of Waterbeer Street negotiated a 999 year lease for a site that is now the Dissenters' Graveyard, but what was then a tract outside the city walls. By ordinance, Non-Conformists were not allowed to be buried inside the City walls. A Jewish cemetery was located just a short distance away, also outside the walls.

Over the centuries the site fell into disuse, and became a jumble of rotting tombs, weeds and debris. In 2014 grants from numerous trusts and private donations permitted the total renovation and reconstruction of the area. I was fortunate enough to visit there in 2016, to have met the people who spearheaded and conducted the renovation, and now count Yvonne Hensman among my dearest friends.

Among these people was a lovely, and brilliant gentleman named Martin Deyer, an amazing and meticulous archeologist who explained so much to me in layman's terms, about the type and construction of the tombs and headstones. Beryl Coe, Gordon Read and Ian M. Varndell compiled a pamphlet called *"Exeter Dissenters' Graveyard: A brief history of a Georgian burial ground from 1748 to 2018."* It provides a thorough and colorful picture of the cemetery and its history.

When I saw the Graveyard it was months away from its opening to the public. Some of the tombs were still being repaired, grass was being planted, and the path had been repaired. A bench would soon be placed on the back wall, and an explanatory plaque erected near the front gate on Magdalen Street.

The amazing sense of and care for their history is apparent in the research and physical labor that have "resurrected" this cemetery. The National Lottery Fund and private donations and much physical labor have resulted in an amazing remembrance of people to whom we are related… people who lived 300 years ago.

Just inside the gate and to the right, the grave beside which I am standing, is the resting place of William Gifford but there is no date. Farther along on the left hand side is a more elaborate tomb which is surrounded by a wrought iron fence. The Architectural survey bears the name of Ann Gifford, and the date 1767/8. She is a great aunt.

THE GIFFORDS OF EXETER

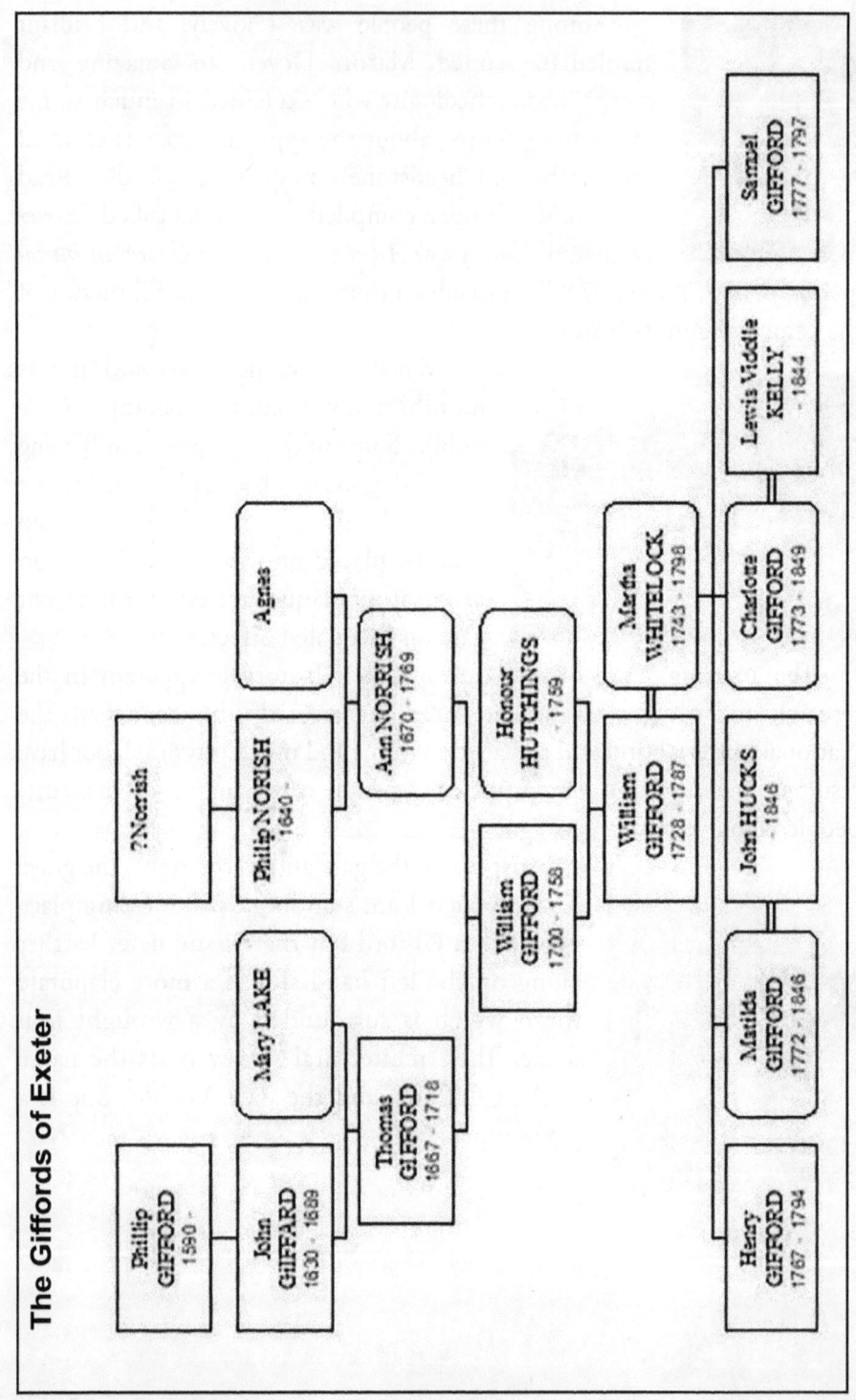

6
THE FAMILY

Following is a list of direct ancestors, husbands and wives, with known birth, marriage and death dates as well as the number of their will if it is in the appendix. Also included are the will of one uncle (Wearman Gifford) and one marriage settlement (Ann Kelly).

John Gifford (will, appendix I)
(c1590 – 6/8/1689)
Married ?
Mary Lake

Thomas Gifford (will, appendix II)
(? – 11/11/1718)
Married 14 June 1692
Ann Norrish (? – 1769) (will, appendix III)

William Gifford (will, appendix IV)
(9/17/1700 – 1757)
Married 2/5/1723/4
Honour Hutchings (? – 1759) (will, appendix V)

William Gifford (will, appendix VI)
(1728 – 1787/88)
Did Not Marry
Martha Whitelock (? – 1798) (will, appendix VII)

Charlotte Gifford (will, appendix VIII)
(1773 – 1849)
Married 1794
Lewis Kelly, Cornet Of The 8th Reg't of 12th Dragoons (no will found)
(? – 1844)

Ann Kelly
(? – 1859) (marriage settlement, appendix IX)
Married 1840
Waldron Kelly (1817 – 1853) (no will found)

Wearman Gifford (will, appendix X)
(1774 – 1836)

7
JOHN GIFFORD
c1630 – 1688

But let us stop here, and meet our first English ancestors, follow them from their humble roots to their success in the Exeter we have just described, and then connect them to "*The Kellys of Kildare.*" Much of the information is culled from their wills which are in the Appendices.

The earliest English ancestors were from families called Norrish and Gifford, residents of the County of Somerset in the Southwest of England, a beautiful landscape of rolling hills and flat lands for farming. A land that saw Roman settlements as well as much earlier civilizations. The first

records of the Norrish family are of a couple named Phillip and Agnes who farmed in the village of Culmstock. Through birth records of their four daughters we can estimate their own birth dates at somewhere between 1630 and 1640. (*King Charles I was beheaded in 1630, and Cromwell took over as Lord Protector. These were turbulent times.*)

The fertile land provided sustenance for farmers and herders alike. One feature of the long-ago land that our Norrish family must have known is still to be seen on a high hill on Blackdown Common. Medieval or sixteenth century in origin, the beehive shaped Culmstock Beacon is one of a chain of Elizabethan hill stations used for lighting fires to warn of advancing enemies such as the Spanish Armada. It crumbled and was rebuilt in

1870, but it was clearly there, and in use, in our ancestors' day. A good imagination can easily picture farmer Phillip Norrish and his wife Ann gathering the family about them as the fire burned bright in the dark night sky, signaling an unnamed threat.

The Giffords lived in neighboring Somerset, in a town called Wellington, a rural area, whose history is traceable to pre-historic, and Anglo Saxon settlements. Wellington was chartered as a town in 1215, became a center for trade during the Middle Ages, and in 1548 was sold to Edward Seymour, brother of Henry VIII's beloved, though short lived third wife, Jane. A Historical Society booklet relates that in 1600 the town consisted of 6 serfs, 16 villains (villagers), 6 stallholders (farmers) and information about the extent of plowable fields. It is quite possible that there were Gifford ancestors in Wellington and its close surroundings as far back as imagination can run.

Our Gifford's records begin with just the name 'Thomas' who is listed as father of John the Elder a yeoman. John and his wife, Mary Lake, raised at least four children; William, Samuel, John and Thomas, our direct ancestor, whose June 30, 1616 baptismal record names his father as John Gifford. Though it cannot be certain from just the names on the baptismal record that this John is indeed the father of our Thomas Gifford, an item in John's will (appendix I) and a similar item in Thomas's will (appendix II) eliminates any doubt that indeed our very first Gifford ancestor was born in Wellington sometime in the late 1500's. probably about 1590. *(Elizabeth I was Queen of England from 1558 – 1603, during the first 10 or 15 years of our ancestor's lifetime!)*

That will includes the ownership of "... a Close of Land commonly known by the name of Ditchford Close lying in the parish of Wellington. .." which John bequeathed to his son Thomas. The same land figures again in Thomas's will when he bequeaths it to his son William in 1718.

John Gifford's last will and testament as extracted from the Registry of the Lord Bishop of Bath and Wells, is dated the "eighth day of June in the year of our Lord 1688 and is now held in the *Registry of the Consistorial Court of Wills.*" The will extract also mentions a second son, Stephen who would inherit Ditchford Close if Thomas or the "Heirs Male of his body and lawfully begotten" were not available. I have not found a birth or baptismal record for Stephen. Since this is only an extraction, there were surely other

items in the original will, but for now all we know is that Thomas, as the first born son, inherited the land. In an agrarian society like this, probably only land was considered important enough to be included in the extract. But it leaves us without the names of other legatees and interesting views of their lives, possessions and values.

This modern photo of Ditchford Close surely captures the beauty of the land when John was raising his sons in exactly the same place three hundred years ago.

8
THOMAS GIFFORD
c1616 – 1688

Our Gifford line continues with John's son Thomas who was born in 1616. *Queen Elizabeth I had died and her first cousin twice removed, James I was king).* Young Thomas married Ann Norrish of Culmstock Parish, a center of weaving and wool trades, on 14 June 1692 in Wellington. They had five children, sons William and Phillip, and daughters Sarah, Mary and Ann.

Thomas' will (appendix II) which was proved at his death in 1718 reveals that he was a wealthy man who left a large estate. In addition to £1,770 in specific bequests to his sons and daughters, he left numerous estates including Ditchford Meadows which he bequeathed to his son William. This is the property which solidified the paternal link to John, and will feature in other family transactions in later generations.

Thomas appointed his wife Ann his executrix. He willed land in West Buckland to his son Philip, £500 to each of his daughters, and £10 pounds each when they reached twenty one years to Mary, Joan and Ann, the three children of his daughter Mary Gifford Buncombe. Thomas bequeathed gold pieces to his brother John and his sister, and he directed that £3 be set aside for the poor. This largess was to be distributed by his wife Ann who was also appointed to select deserving poor families, each of which would receive six shillings. It is a very interesting document.

Thomas' wife Ann outlived her husband by fifty years and was a woman of property when she died in 1769.

Her will (appendix III) is fascinating in its detailed bequests to her children, daughters in law, grandchildren, great grandchildren and friends. The details included the disposal of not only her finest clothing, "best suit of linning and Black Silk gown" but also her "common wearing apparel."

Grandchildren generally inherited £100, great grandchildren (born and yet to be conceived) £10. There are also payments of interest and much specific direction.

At some point between her first will and the codicil that was added two years later, Ann must have gotten very angry with her granddaughter Honour, as the Codicil directs that the executor ". ... revoke and absolutely make void the said Legacy of two hundred pounds to the said Honour Norman." I wonder why! Mother, Grandmother, Great-grandmother, Mother-in-Law and friend, Ann Norrish Gifford was quite a lady. I'd have liked to have known her. She certainly knew her own mind and strictly controlled her assets even from the grave.

In 1711, eight years before his father's death, Thomas and Ann's son William was apprenticed to Anthony Vicary, Sr. of Exeter, Grocer. With this move of fifty miles to the south, the Gifford lines began their march from farmer and yeoman to grocer to merchant to doctor in our direct line, and barrister and Baron in the extended line.

9
WILLIAM GIFFORD
1700 – 1757

Of this William, more is known. He was born in Wellington on the ninth of September, 1700, and during his 58 year lifetime saw five different monarchs in England, *(King William III and Queen Mary, Queen Ann, Queen Anne, King George I and King George II)*. William was apprenticed to a grocer in Exeter in 1711, and his papers not only still exist, but they are online from the National Archives.

Britain, Country Apprentices 1710 – 1808 Transcription

First name	William
Last name	Gifford
Role	apprentice
Indenture or registration year	1711
Indenture year	1711
Premium	£0 0s 0d
Place	Wellington
Apprentice's first name	William
Apprentice's last name	Gifford
Apprentice's place	Wellington
Apprentice's county	Somerset
Apprentice's parent first name	Thomas
Master's first name	Anthony
Master's last name	Vicary(Senior)
Master's occupation	Grocer
Master's place	Exeter
Master's county	Devon
National Archives Ref.	(IR 1 series) 43 r 33

Society of Genealogists vol.	11
Society of Genealogists page	2180
Society of Genealogists number	80137
Record type	*Records*
Record set	*Britain, country apprentices 17*
Subcategory	*Education and work*
Subcategory	*Apprentices*

Collections from UK Society of Genealogists
(Find My Past.com transcription of the original record.)

When his apprenticeship ended, and his money saved, he married Honor Hutchings on February 5, 1723 in Moreton Hampstead, Devon and began to raise a family in Exeter where he did business. Their first child was a daughter called Ann, and after five years of marriage, their first son William was born on 24th of October, 1728 in Devon.

Two more sons, George and John are mentioned in William's will, (appendix IV) as well as Ann who is called by her married name Ann Fryer, wife of John Fryer, Merchant. A son called Samuel was born on the 13th of July 1740, but is not mentioned in the will., suggesting that he was no longer alive. It is interesting that the name Samuel was that of John and Mary Gifford's son born in 1620 – a great uncle of this Samuel.

William's very impressive fortune was based on profits from trade and sound investments in Bonds and in real estate. It began slowly, with his work in the family business, but within ten years after his marriage, he was earning enough to hire his own apprentice. According to a document in the National Archives, in 1733 William hired his first six year apprentice, Mark Sealy whose family paid a fee of between £100 and £400 for the privilege. When Mark's term was over or nearly over, Samuel Parminter signed on in 1739. Fifteen years later John Fryer (who would become his son in law) began his apprenticeship, and 5 years after that, in 1759, John Shorland became William's last recorded apprentice. William and Honour's son George was an apprentice when his father died, though I do not know if he apprenticed with his father's Partnership or with another. I have not found his name on the lists.

When William died in 1758, after 29 years of marriage, his thriving business appears to have been continued by John Fryer, his daughter's husband, his one-time apprentice. This was often done, both to keep the family business in the hands of the knowledgeable men, and to find appropriate husbands for daughters. There was quite enough capital left for his first son to become a Doctor of Physic rather than a merchant, and for his widow, Honour, to live in comfort until her death seven years later.

Another interesting historical note is that we only have this amazing apprenticeship document because in an effort to raise money, the government levied a tax, called a Stamp Tax, on all such documents. All taxes were registered with the government, and the tax rolls are still available in the Archives, and now online. This was the not the same Stamp Act that galvanized the colonists in Boston into dumping tea. The apprenticeship tax was one of string of taxes that the British government regularly levied on all sorts of things and goods when the civil coffers were low.

As with his ancestors, William's will is the device by which we best know him. The first item, beyond the pious, is the disposal of the lands of Dursay's Farm Dolways and Ditchford in Wellington to his elder son William Gifford along with two hundred pounds.

His son John received two thousand pounds, in order to make himself "equal partnership in trade" with his mother, until son "George's apprenticeship shall expire". The will further states that if George were still an apprentice at the time of his father's death, his mother, William's widow Honour, would be entrusted with the operation of the business, thereby holding a place for George, and running the business with her son John. I am not sure if there were other relatives in the "Partnership" as it is referred to in Honour's will, or just the immediate family. I am not sure if such financial power was usually given to women.

As is common to all the wills, there are detailed provisions for every eventuality in an era of serious illness resulting in death of the young and the old. William leaves his daughter Ann Fryer interest on bonds etc. which shall be administered by a William Clarke, and paid to Ann annually. This money was to be paid "during her natural life for her separate use exclusive of her said husband so that he shall have no power or control over the same nor shall the same be subject to his debts or Engagements." At her death Anne's children were to receive the remains of the estate.

Thomas did stipulate that with the permission of the administrators, Ann could use her money to provide a 'natural child of her body' with the monies needed to purchase an apprenticeship. This will was signed on January 8, 1753, four years before his death. Thomas added a codicil on December 12, 1753, wherein he stated that he had already given his son John the £2500 and *"after his death, the house he now lives in as a recognition of his marriage to Mrs. Anna Lee."* This branch of the family, though not ours, is very interesting and will be discussed in a later chapter.

John's first wife, Anna Lee Gifford lived for 13 years after the marriage during which time she bore three children. Nine years later, John Gifford married Dorothy Wearman who would bear five children, the youngest of whom, Robert, would become the Solicitor General of England, Lord Gifford 1st Baron of St Leonard's and Master of the Rolls. The rise of "Trade" in our own extended family! *(At this time the title , which has gone through nephews as well and sons, is still in the family. Anthony, the 6th Lord Gifford is an attorney who divides his time between London and Jamaica)*

10
HONOUR HUTCHINGS GIFFORD
– 1759

Here is an interesting woman. She left her parents, a brother and three sisters, when she married and moved thirty five miles away with her new husband, William. She must have been a worldly and enterprising woman for her time since her husband, (via his will) thought her a capable, stand-in partner for his business as she waited for his younger son to finish his apprenticeship. William's will indicated that when George finished his internship, she, Honour, was to step aside. Reading her will (appendix V) presents a very different picture.

She begins by giving £300 to son their John, and £20 each to his sons John, George and William. She gives £600 for her Daughter Ann, though it is in the management of her brothers William and John. She also gives *"unto my said Daughter Fryer all my wearing apparel and my Gold watch and my best Diamond Ring and my Silver Waiter (a tray) marked AGHG May 21 1737, and a Silver Tankard"* Lovely and interesting to know that she had more than one diamond ring. She then indemnifies William and John as executors.

In the next, very curious part of the will, Honour mentions her youngest son, George for the first time. She wills him seven hundred pounds payable within three months after her death. She then refers to her 'dear' late husband's will wherein he stipulates that from the time of his death to the end of George's apprenticeship *"my said husband's Trade and Business should be carried on my me and soon as our said son George's apprenticeship should expire I should not from that time be any further concerned in the said <u>Trade and my share should cease for the benefit of our son George by our son John.</u>"*

But in the very next sentence Honour "directs and appoints that *" my said son George shall not be entitled to receive the said legacy of seven hundred pounds . . ."* until he legally renounces all claims on the partnership."[underlining mine] Did she just disinherit her son, notwithstanding the contents of his father's will? If so, it is amazing that a woman of those times could have so much financial power. I wonder what he did to merit such a decision? Did he not finish the apprenticeship? Or did she like being a partner? But then, in the next sentence she wills store's counters and shelves to John and scales and weights to George. So… perhaps if he needs scales and weights, he must be in business somewhere? With her and John? Elsewhere? Who knows! Yvonne Hensman thinks that he just hadn't shown any interest in Trade. But then she leaves him scales and weights. Another unsolved puzzle.

Honour goes on. She wills £5 a year to her brother Thomas. (Is this a thoughtful gesture or a slap in the face?), then £10 each and her 'common wearing apparel" to her sisters, and £10 to her servant . The task of separating the "common" from the "best" wearing apparel is left to her daughter in law. That must have been a thankless task. The rest of her belongings of any kind and her belongings from her husband's estate are willed to her son and executor, William.

The ladies Gifford are a strong lot! Honour only lived for a year longer than her husband. So to find out what happened, we have to look to the wills in the next generation. And there we will find even more surprises.

11
WILLIAM GIFFORD
1728 – 1787/8

Though he was the eldest son of William and Honour Gifford, he did not enter the family business. He became a Doctor of Physic and left the linen shop and business to his mother and brothers. Because he did receive his share of their assets in their wills, there did not seem to be any animus on the part of his parents, so I am led to believe that his choice of profession met with their approval.

Medicine in the 1700's was vastly different from medicine today or even in the eighteenth or nineteenth centuries. The medical profession in England in the 1700's was in a state of flux. Its practitioners were transforming from the ragtag medieval barbers who pulled teeth, the herbalists, and the surgeon/butchers, many of whom were charlatans, into aspiring professionals, with guilds, apprenticeships, and degree programs at a few universities. Royal Colleges of Medicine existed in London, Edinburgh, Aberdeen, Cambridge, Oxford, Leyden, Reims and Dublin.

Unfortunately, we have not been able to find William Gifford on any lists of graduates, but because of his use of the title, I originally suspected that William Gifford was, indeed, a university graduate Doctor of Medicine. Two other Exeter medical practitioners are mentioned in various contemporary histories, including the comment that one was building a fine new house. But both of these men are called Surgeons.

It was only when researching William's youngest half-brother, an attorney who rose to national prominence, that I learned that this youngest sibling did not have a University or Public School education. If he did not, then the absence of William's name from the university records is no accident. William Gifford was a Doctor of Physic, presumably trained by apprenticeship, and not a University educated Doctor of Medicine.

Curious to know what our ancestor did in his daily practice, I searched Google for medical history in eighteenth century England, and found amazing and bizarre things that were said to be a step above the medieval. I presume that Dr. Gifford used much the same remedies. A man called Dr. William Cullen, one of the most famous physicians and professors at Edinburgh University, a man who daringly lectured in English rather than Latin, was consulted by the famous Biographer Samuel Johnson. To Johnson's list of complaints and symptoms, Dr. Cullen responded:

> "I am sorry to find that there is so little in the power of Physic. . . to be done for him. At the age of 74 Asthma and Dropsy are very insurmountable distempers. For the first I have found the most useful remedies to be Blistering, issues and especially gentle vomits." He goes on to say that he is glad that Johnson "is using Laudanum" and recommends "the vinegar of Squills…" But ultimately, Dr. Cullen is pessimistic about Johnson's chances of surviving another year, because "I suspect that he has not only water in his limbs but also in his breast." *(Healio.com)*

A quick search of the medical terms reveals that Asthma was probably any throat or lung disease, and its remedy, "blistering" is the application of a "Spanish Fly," a beetle, to the affected spot, from which a "healing" blister resulted. This treatment was used on George Washington on his death bed. Laudanum and opium were used regularly. Dropsy was swelling in any part of the body, probably caused by congestive heart failure. For that, Dr. Johnson used Squills, a Mediterranean area plant whose bulb was mashed, added to vinegar, left to brew for a week, and then drunk by patients.

If famous Dr. Cullen charged two guineas for a consultation ($400 in 2020), and less for widows, students and clerics, we can assume that our Exeter Doctor of Physic, William Gifford, made a decent if smaller living in addition to his inherited wealth, investments and property. His will (appendix VI) makes it quite clear that he was a man of means. He left £460 to enable his son Henry to purchase a commission in the army as an ensign, the entry level officer rank.

William left £450 to his son Samuel, £500 each to his daughters Matilda and Charlotte on Trust for their use, but managed by Thomas Gifford of Ford in Somerset, George Gifford of Exeter and John Bowring of the Parish of Saint Leonard's. In addition to cash and shares, William Gifford owned a house on Friernhay Street, near the North Gate, almost a mile from the Dissenters' Graveyard. Conveniently, there was a hospital in Friernhay Street.

He also left each of his younger children a third share in "my said Lands Tenements and Hereditaments". A google search reveals that Lands means the dirt and anything on or under it; Tenements are any structures attached to the land; and Hereditaments are any interests in real estate capable of being inherited. Messuage is another word in many of the wills, and it means the dwelling house and its adjacent buildings and land.

In other wills in the family, the children mentioned are usually referred to as "my son" or "my said son;" "My Daughter," or "my said Daughter." But this one is different. William's will reads, "I give and bequeath unto *my natural or reputed son commonly called or known by the name of* Henry Gifford…" The format is repeated in the case of each of the four children. Later in the will, after specific bequests to Henry, he appoints the same gentlemen to pay and apply rents and profits "*toward the maintenance and education of my other natural or reputed children commonly called or known by the names of Samuel Gifford Matilda Gifford and Charlotte Gifford.*" Why the repeated and unusual appellation of "natural or reputed children"?

If his profession was a departure from family tradition, it was not the only departure. William was not legally married to Martha Whitelock, the mother of his children, but she was both executor of and a beneficiary in his will. Martha's own will describes her as 'Spinster,' and her surname is Whitelock. The only document that refers to her as Martha Gifford is the entry in the "Appendix to the Parochial registers of St. Leonard's Parish."

1794 Feb.10 Lewis Kelly, now of Exeter, Esq. and Charlotte Gifford, of St. Leonard's , a minor, with the consent of Martha Gifford, her mother, Witnesses, Matilda and Anna Maria Gifford.

In this one instance, in the church record, she was known as Martha Gifford. But legally she was not. What was she called by the shopkeepers and friends? Why would such a proper citizen not marry the mother of his known and acknowledged children? It doesn't seem possible, and so I have sought an explanation.

The one possibility that I can invest with even a little credulity, is that it had something to do with religion. But even then there are two possibilities. Strict Non-Conformists did at times refuse to participate in Church of England ceremonies, but wed in unrecognized and unrecorded Non-Conformist ceremonies. But the Bow meeting kept extensive records of births, marriages and deaths, so that possibility is very unlikely.

The other possible religious explanation is that the parties were of different religions. And that is in fact true. Though Christian, in this hotbed of religious intolerance in England, it mattered enormously that one was Non-Conformist or Church of England, the other not. Martha Whitelock was from an Anglican family, baptized into the Church of England. Perhaps her religious beliefs prevented her from a participating in a Non-Conformist wedding, and perhaps William's religious scruples and social position prevented him marrying in her church. She was not buried in the Non-Conformist Graveyard on Magdalen the one at Moretonhampstead.

Another remote possibility is that Martha, who was about fifteen years younger than William, might have been from a different class and therefore deemed unsuitable to the Giffords or to the Bow Meeting. But the Gifford family does not appear to have objected, as prominent Gifford relatives were her trustees, executors and advisors, as was John Bowring, a very prominent member of the town and the Bow Meeting. Children of all the Gifford branches appear to have been on good terms, and claimed relationship with one another.

There had to have been an explanation. 'Good Non-Conformist girls did not have four recognized children out of wedlock with members of prominent families.' The Doctor had no other family, and recognized only his four children and Martha in his will.

What becomes abundantly clear, is that William Gifford and Martha Whitelock did not want to appear in any records, except where their property was concerned.

12
MARTHA WHITELOCK
1743 – 1798

Most of what we know about Martha is inextricably linked with William Gifford and their unusual circumstances that have already been discussed in the previous chapter. There is only a little more to add about one of the most puzzling of all the "Gifford women". She was born in Crediton, Devon on 5 November 1743, and had a twin sister called Mary. Ancestry.com displays transcriptions of both birth records, with only their names, dates, and parents' names. No church is mentioned. The Biblical significance of the paired names surely signifies religious parents. Martha was the woman who kept busy with domestic affairs while her sister Mary sat rapt at the feet of the Lord. The Bible says that Mary had chosen the better path. Hmmm. How did Martha like her name? Did it in any way determine her role?

Only because Yvonne Hensman had access to other sources do we have the sisters' complete baptismal records, which are Church of England, not Non-Conformist. We know for certain that the Whitelock family was Anglican. Of all the possible explanations for the unusual situation, that one best explains her lack of a marriage to William Gifford, the Non-Conformist who was fifteen years her senior.

It is possible to know that they had four children because they each dutifully and carefully wrote wills to protect and dispense their property, but impossible to know the exact dates of the births or baptisms of any of their four children, since not one of them is recorded anywhere – not in the files of Ancestry, Find My Past, Family Search, British Newspapers or the UK National Archives. Doctor William and Spinster Martha simply did not ever register or sacramentalize anything.

But there are enough clues to make an educated guess about birth order and dates. Cemetery plaques date their children's' births between 1767 and 1777 – Henry, Matilda, Charlotte and Stephen.

Martha's will (appendix VII) was executed on the 18th day of February, 1795, with a codicil on the same day. By then she would have received notification of Henry's death in Martinique in 1794. She now had two married daughters, and a twenty one year old unmarried son. She first leaves ten guineas each to her niece, Mary Whitelock (a child of a brother who I have not yet identified) and to Harriet, daughter of John Gifford (William's brother's child). She leaves twenty guineas to George Gifford of Exeter, dyer and counterman, and twenty guineas to John Bowring.

Sometime before her marriage, Martha and her daughter Matilda executed some sort of bond with the huge linen merchants Barings Short and Cole of Exeter, whereby Matilda is to be paid interest which is carefully shielded from access by her husband. In the way of Gifford ladies, Martha Whitelock entails this money for the "issue of Matilda's body," to prevent John Hucks from appropriating any of it, even after his wife's death. Martha appoints George Gifford and John Bowring trustees of these assets after her death.

She again appoints George Gifford and John Bowring to be executors and Trustees of the rest of her estate for the benefit of her three surviving children, also making certain that the Charlotte's funds are protected from use of her new husband, the Anglican Irishman, Lewis Kelly, Cornet of the 12th Regiment of the Eight Dragoons, the Prince of Wales' own Royal Lancers. Cornet is the entry level officer rank in this very respectable regiment.

Codicils in previous wills indicated changes, but this one appears to have been inserted to correct an inadvertent omission, as the dates are the same and the bequests minor. Martha wills ten guineas to Dorothy (Wearman) Gifford, "as a mark of my regard for her." At this time Dorothy would have been married to William's widowed brother John Gifford for about six years, would have had two sons of her own, and been stepmother to the four children of John's first wife Anna Lee Gifford. Those four children included Charlotte's 'not-husband', William.

13
WILLIAM & MARTHA'S CHILDREN
HENRY, MATILDA, CHARLOTTE, SAMUEL

Because there are no birth or baptismal records for any of them, it is an entertaining puzzle on a rainy Covid 19, July 2020 day to email with wonderful researcher Yvonne Hensman in Exeter and to try to figure out the children's birth order and possible birth dates, given the records that we do have. Those records include engravings on two memorial plaques in the Dissenters' Graveyard, one for Henry and one for Samuel; the wills of both William and Martha; and the marriage records of Martha and Charlotte.

Henry's plaque states that he died in 1794 at age 27. Therefore he was born in 1767, and was 20 or 21 years old at the time of his father's death in 1787. It is not possible to be certain that the Henry Gifford who I found in the 70th Regiment of Foot, was actually our Henry Gifford, but all circumstantial evidence points that way. I believe that two years after his Father's death in 1789/90, he purchased a £460 Ensign's commission in the 70th Regiment of Foot, and two years later sold it and purchased a Lieutenant's commission in the same regiment. This was the usual avenue for promotion.

The deployments of the 70th fit the story of our Henry. It was on Garrison duty in "Ireland mainly Dublin" from 1790 to 1793 where Henry could easily have met and befriended a fellow British officer of similar age and rank, Lewis Kelly.

But in 1793 the 70th deployed to the West Indies, to fight the French. In the Battle of Martinique, which lasted from February 5th to the 24 of March, 900 French troops were pitted against 6,000 British soldiers, 3 ships of the line and 5 frigates. Add to those odds, the fact that the French planters on Martinique were actively helping the British, and there is no question of who would win the day. There were losses in the battle, and many more casualties to yellow fever and malaria.

A historical note on one reason for English success in the war in these French Caribbean colonies... France, as part of its Revolution, had simultaneously outlawed slavery both at home and in its territories. But England had not. Therefore, the French planters in Martinique and Guadeloupe aided the English and fought for an English victory, so that their slaves would not be freed, and their sugar cane based fortunes not lost.

A family note ... Henry's sister Charlotte's wedding in Exeter took place on February 10, the same month and year as Henry's death. An ocean away, in a time when messages took months to reach across that ocean, his mother and siblings did not know that he was dead.

The second brother, Samuel Gifford's memorial stone states that he died in 1797 aged 20 years, therefore he was born in 1777. He would have been 17 years old in the year when his brother died and his sisters married. Beryl Coe has determined that he died in Bermuda, another British colony. Unfortunately, no evidence has been found to let us know if he too, was a member of the military, or if he was there as part of a trip perhaps relating to the family's mercantile business. His mother's will directs the reallocation of his share of the family fortune.

Determining the birth dates of the sisters is a little more challenging. It is my belief that Matilda is older than Charlotte. They were born between their brothers.

Ten years separate the births of the brothers – 1767–1777. If we subtract two years on each end for spacing between children, the girls must have been born between 1769–1775. I presume that Matilda was 21 at Charlotte's wedding in order to be a witness, and I know that Charlotte was under 21, Therefore Matilda is the elder.

But, in the 1841 English census (which rounded ages to 5 or 0) a then widowed Matilda will give her age as 65, giving her a birth date of 1773–76. There is no way to know for certain. Again presuming two years between births, with a possible miscarriage in between, my "best guess" is Matilda (c1771 – 1846) or 1776 – 1846) and Charlotte (c1774 – 1849).

There are two other clues to my theory of their birth order, and they are first, the fact that Matilda was named executrix of her brother's 1789 will (she had to have been 18). Second, the fact that she is mentioned and dealt with before her sister in both her father's and her mother's wills. The usual practice in wills was to mention sons first, daughters second - both in order of seniority within the family.

There are some charming and some poignant personal things that can be discerned from the documents. The answer to the question of how a 17 year old girl in Exeter happened to be marrying a soldier from Dublin, is surely to be explained by examining the military annuls. When Ensign Henry Gifford was sent to "Dublin in the Kingdom of Ireland," he might easily have met a fellow British soldier, Cornet Lewis Kelly and perhaps visited his Dublin home and the family estates in Kildare. Or perhaps the young soldiers met in Exeter. Lewis' arrival in Exeter was probably military because the marriage record describes him as "now of the city of Exeter". But he was obviously taken with his friend's little sister. The families seem to have been social equals, and her mother was Church of England, so there was no obstacle other than the bride's being willing to move to "wild Ireland." But she was young.....

Matilda Hucks lived ten years longer than her husband John. Their beautiful home, Foxdown, was described in an earlier chapter. His brief will (not included here), was proved in 1836, and quite simply left everything to her, his heir and executrix. They appear to have had no children. But Matilda will be an important person in the life of at least one of Charlotte's children, her niece, Mary Kelly.

And now the poignant, or sad part of this story. 1794 was a year of dramatic change in Martha's life. William had been dead for seven years, and her family was breaking apart. Henry was dead in Martinique, Charlotte was married living in Kildare, in Ireland, and her sister Martha had married and moved to Foxdown, still in Devon, but not an easy journey at that time. She was alone. There is absolutely no clue as to what she did or where she lived for most of the next four years until her death in April 1798. Her will was made in Exeter, so presumably she lived in the house where she had always lived.... But perhaps she went to live with Matilda. Surely she didn't join Charlotte in Ireland. In the next chapter it will be very apparent why she did not. Since Charlotte is our direct ancestor, she deserves a chapter of her own.

14
CHARLOTTE GIFFORD
c1775 – 1849

We have described Charlotte's stable Exeter birthplace, seen the oddity of her parents' arrangement, though we do not know if the children and the community in general were aware of it. We have some understanding of the middle-class lifestyle and social position the Gifford family enjoyed. We also have looked at the instability of the monarchy in earlier periods, but George III had been on the throne for 20 years before Charlotte was born and would reign for many years thereafter.

The American colonies were causing trouble, and the French Revolution had given people "notions," but all in all it was a time of prosperity. England's power and prestige rose after the spectacular victories of Lord Nelson at Trafalgar in 1805, and Lord Nelson at Waterloo in 1815. King George III's increasing episodes of madness would not necessitate a regency until 1811.

Charlotte and Lewis began their married life in Exeter, where their first child, Mary, was baptized on the December 23, 1794, at St. Leonard's, the church where they were married. It was a tragic Christmas for the young couple when Mary died three days later on the 26th. Only because of this one record, we know that they stayed in Exeter for at least a year.

We don't know where they lived in 1795 and 1796 – either peaceful Exeter, or the hornet's nest of rebellion in wild, dangerous Ireland. And what of their life together? By 1797 they were in Kildare where civil unrest, rebellion, death, property burning, and spying awaited them. Lewis and his father were involved with the rebel group of United Men in Kildare. An outline of the major events in Ireland's next 50 turbulent years, the years of Charlotte's marriage, will help to set the stage.

1795   The Orange Order, group of Protestant Northern Irishmen, was founded to insure the Protestant ascendancy in the face of Roman Catholic demands for emancipation.
1791   The Society of the United Irishmen, inspired by the French Revolution, founded by Presbyterians, but including Catholics, attempted to ensure equality to all Irishmen. Originally peaceful, it turned to violent action.
1798   Involvement of some of the Kelly family.
1798   Rebellion of 1798 led by Wolfe Tone, a Dublin lawyer
        Rebellions throughout Ireland, many in Kildare
        Damage to Kelly property in Kildare, deaths
        Defeat of the United Irishmen at Vinegar Hill
1829   Catholic Emancipation and riots
1845, 1846,1847,1848,1849   The Great Famine

Two sources help to date their time in Kildare. The first is the book called *Kildare in '98* by Paedar Mac Suibhne. Leinster Leader Ltd. 1978, and second is a series of baptismal records in the Cathedral Church in Kildare.

Mac Suibhne's book places Lewis Kelly in Kildare in 1789, and not in a flattering way. Both Catholics and Protestants were in an organization called the United Men. Its members, both Protestant and Catholic sought to unite in their demand for real independence for Ireland. The Crown violently objected and had spies in that organization and visa-versa. Quoting Bishop Comerford, "Thomas Kelly of Madddenstown [Lewis' Father] is supposed to know *everything* relative to the business of the United Men. His son, Lewis Kelly, is concerned with them and might easily be prevailed upon to make a discovery, [squeal, rat, spy] being a man of weak nerves and a great drunkard." Poor Charlotte.

They survived the Revolution, and settled down to raise a very large family surrounded by the numerous members of the prosperous Kelly clan. Lewis's rents and inheritance as well as Charlotte's supported them well in an area of Ireland that was blessed with rich soil, and not far from Dublin. Charlotte's 1833 will names 10 surviving children, six girls and four boys. Catherine, Charlotte, Eliza, Mary, Matilda, Anne and the boys Thomas, Lewis, William, and Henry. There were also the first Mary and the first

Matilda who was born in Kildare on October 14, 1801 and died ten days later, therefore at least 12 pregnancies.

After 50 years of marriage, Louis died on October 11, 1844. His funeral was held in Kildare Cathedral, but it is clearly stated in the record book of the Cathedral that he was buried elsewhere. I have never found his grave. Unfortunately, his will was almost certainly burned in the fire in Dublin in 1922. Five years later Charlotte died not in Ireland, not in her native Exeter, but in Carnarvon, Wales. One more "Why" in a Gifford story.

Fortunately, her 1833 will (appendix VIII) was proved in London, rather than Ireland, and a copy exists in the National Archives. More simple than many of the others, it first recalls the settlement made before her marriage in 1794 in which the power over her personal assets is "reserved and vested to me of giving and bequeathing lands and money thereon settled...after the death of my husband to and amongst the children of the said marriage..." She goes on to mention £1812.7.3 now vested at 3 1/2%, and £303.15 bank stock to be equally divided among her six daughters, and directs that the sums be paid to them on the day of their marriages or when the youngest child reaches the age of 21 years. (Each share would have been about £425). Should one die, her moneys would be divided among the other sisters.

In Charlotte's will her sons are dealt with second. After funeral expenses, she directs that her remaining assets are to be handled as follows. Her son Thomas was well provided for in his grandfather's will, and so his mother leaves him five guineas to purchase a ring as a token of her maternal regard. The remainder will be divided into three parts, and paid to Lewis, William and Henry Kelly as they reach 21 years of age. John Hucks of Foxdown in Devon England, her sister's husband, is appointed executor and custodian of the funds. The witnesses are not the usual family members, since she is in Wales or in Ireland. They are Robert, Evan and William Roberts.

Following is a notation from after Charlotte's death. It states that her assets had been distributed except for £400 @3% annuities, and the fourth part of a piece of real estate from William Gifford, Doctor of Physic. By this time, her brother-in-law and executor John Hucks had died, and was replaced by Mary Kelly, Spinster and Charlotte Kelly, the youngest of Charlotte's children, who will serve as co-executors.

And what of her other children? In fact, I have almost no information about Thomas, other than one possible reference in the Great Britain War Office Registers 1772 – 1935 which lists a Thomas Kelly, born in 1798 in Kildare who was in service in Berhampore, Bengal, India on December 4, 1828. Military service is very much in family tradition, so this is possible, but not provable.

A Lewis Kelly owns property in Rathangan and Feighcullen, Kildare both before and well after Lewis Sr.'s death, so this is likely Charlotte's son, living in Kildare among his relatives, and close to his mother. I have no idea what happened to William, as there are just too many William Kellys to even guess. Henry lived to marry. "Henry Kelly Esq., Upper Ormond-Quay, youngest son of the late Lewis Kelly, Esq., Kildare to Judith Mary, daughter of C. Hannan Esq., Kilbalin House, County of Kildare", Nov. 23, 1846. (*Dublin Evening Packet November 28, 1846.*) Upper Ormond-Quay is in Dublin, so this young couple headed to the city in a difficult time.

Just months after Lewis died on the 11th of October 1844, the first blight in the five year horror that was the Potato Famine showed itself in 1845. Though Kildare was not nearly as badly affected as other parts of Ireland, no county or city was spared either the crop failure or the disease and roaming bands of homeless, starving people. I doubt that widowed, English Charlotte would have stayed there. Her son Henry and his wife were in Dublin, as were Ann and her husband, Waldron. Eliza and her husband were in Wales. She had married Owen Poole on 27 January 1827. The Spouse's residence was 'Dwygyfylchi'! The 1841 English Census finds Charlotte's unmarried daughter, 20 year old Mary, living with her widowed 65 year old Aunt Matilda Gifford Hucks at Foxdown, in Parkham. (The custom of 'sharing' children of large families with childless relatives was not at all unusual). In fact, other than 5 guineas for a ring to a favored nephew, Mary eventually inherited all of her Aunt's possessions, including Foxdown.

It has only been a few days since I discovered Eliza's whereabouts, and so answered the nagging question of why Charlotte died in Aber, Caernarvonshire in Wales. Simple, she had run from famine and pestilence to safety and comfort in the home of her daughter. There was a death of an Owen Anthony Pool recorded in Caernarvonshire in 1849. I have no idea if this person was Eliza's husband, so I don't know if Charlotte was also there to comfort a widowed daughter.

15
ANNE KELLY
c1820 – c1858

Anne, the youngest daughter of Charlotte and Lewis Kelly, is another ancestor whose birth, death or baptismal records are nowhere to be found. She is not actually a Gifford of Exeter, but her connection with England was still strong, and she did die in England, so she is here as a transitional figure from *The Giffords of Exeter* to *The Kellys of Kildare*.

We know from Charlotte's will that she was the youngest of the Kelly children. We have the record of her June 8, 1840 marriage to Anson Kelly in the Kildare Cathedral, and we have copies of the many pages of *Griffith's Primary Evaluation of Ireland*. *Griffith's* was a survey done between the years of 1848 and 1864, of every piece of property in Ireland, its occupiers and Lessors size, value and rent, in an effort to rectify unequal tax assessments. When Kildare was surveyed in 1851, at least 20 properties were controlled by Anne Kelly. They included a Female School, a Chapel, a graveyard, a National School, and numerous pieces of land with and without houses and outbuildings. They were among Anne's sources of income.

The property ownership was updated in subsequent years, and in each case, her name bears the notation "In Chancery," or "Reps," indicating that she had died, and that the estate was in legal hands. With those procedures resolved, subsequent records indicate that the properties reverted to the ownership of Lord FitzGerald, the Earl of Kildare. The Public Record Office of Ireland's Index to Probation and Administration lists the 1859 death of an Anne Kelly of Dublin who is almost certainly our ancestor whose will went up in flames along with her husband's in the 1922 Post Office fire.

Perhaps the legal proceedings went badly, or perhaps the lease was for the term of a certain number of lives. But whatever the explanation, there certainly was no more money in that branch of the family. Ann's son Anson came to the United States, penniless, and enlisted as a drummer boy in the Union Army's 17th New York Volunteers in May, 1861. He lived in Camden, New Jersey, but enlisted in New York City because New Jersey wouldn't have him. He was underage. But that is the story of *The Kellys of Kildare*.

These are the lives, as we know them, of men and women whose genes we carry, and whose names we now know, and about whose lives we have some notion. And now we can connect them across the English Channel and follow them to the United States of America.

16
THE PEERAGE

There is only one story left to tell, not of a direct ancestor, but of an uncle and his line. And it is a story that fits perfectly into any history of the Industrial Revolution: the rise of the mercantile class, the ascent of a commoner to the peerage, and the welcome he received. And that is exactly what happened in a branch of our family.

Back in 1769, my 5x great-grandfather gave a house to his second son, John Gifford when he married Anna Lee. Anna lived for a further thirteen years, and bore four sons. At her death, probably from complications of childbirth, her children were John 5, George 4, William 2, and Philip 2 months. Six years later John married Dorothy Wearman. Dorothy gave birth to four more boys and one girl. Wearman in 1773, Thomas in 1775, Charles in 1776, and Robert 1779. The daughter Harriet's birth year is a mystery. There was a 'Harriot' Gifford baptized on 23 May 1794, in the Bow Meeting Church, with John as the father but Deborah, written in beautiful script in the Church book as the mother. The right Harriet ? Probably.

John's business was doing extremely well, and his son George, the only surviving children from his first marriage, joined him in trade. With one exception it appears that the sons of his second marriage were also involved in the business. Wearman Gifford, eldest son of Dorothy, excelled, and became a very wealthy man leaving a legacy of over £30,000 plus securities and two large estates. One, Parkers Well House, came "with the Offices Stables Coachhouse Buildings Gardens Shrubbery and fields belonging thereto." He never married, but cared for his spinster sister Harriet, and for his mother to whom he left an annuity should he predecease her. His will is replete with gifts to charity, the Exeter and Devon Hospital £50; the

Lunatic Asylum £30; The Protestant Dissenters' Charity School £20; Coal Charity £20; and the Deaf and Dumb Institution £20; even the Humane Society £20.. There are many specific bequests to nieces and nephews, to friends, to two servants and even £10 to John Rabson, a shoemaker. Chains, seals, rings gold watches are sprinkled around as well.

But this will has something in it that is really "weird," and illustrates a primal and contemporary fear in a man of wealth and position. I have chosen to include only the wills of direct ancestors, but Wearman's must be an exception. Posterity might think that I've made it up. (appendix X)

Immediately after his name, residence, date and the request that all his debts and funeral expenses be paid, the site (later changed in a codicil) of his chosen cemetery, and the name of the clergyman who should perform the service, he goes on:

> *I request that Mr Samuel Barnes of Exeter may open my body as soon after my death as it can be ascertained that every part of life is extinct and for this service as well as for a mark of my esteem I bequeath to him a legacy of twenty pounds to be paid immediately after my decease.*

He was afraid of being buried alive! Perhaps it did happen from time to time. A coma might have been close enough to death as to be indistinguishable. There were numerous stories about people being buried with a bell tied to their big toe so that should they wake they could ring for help. Wikipedia says that it is not an uncommon phobia, less common now in the days of embalming and cremation, but Wearman was taking no chances. Interesting. You never know what you're going to find in an old will. It is astounding that what you supposed were old wives tales affected your own sophisticated, wealthy, religious family member.

Yvonne Hensman and I differ on our interpretation of this request. She believes that Wearman meant to leave his body to be used in medical research. Body snatching existed during this period when corpses were dug up and sold to the medical profession for their research. Yvonne believes that Wearman was attempting to legitimize the donation of his body. Reader's choice!

One more item from Wearman's will….. tucked in between £20s for a deceased friend's son and £500 and his mother's gold watch to a close friend and associate, there are two further bequests that I found stunning, but have since learned were perfectly ordinary. "To William Roger Bastard of Exeter £50 To his brother Samuel Roger Bastard £50."

My reaction was, "Bastard?" Whose bastard? Friend or relative? William was "Bastard of Exeter" but his brother was only "Bastard"? Did just the elder son receive the title? Bastard couldn't be a last name. Each 'Bastard' received about $8,000. in US 2020. Well, Thanks to Yvonne, once again, I've learned that Bastard certainly is an accepted British surname. This American genealogist is not only grateful for the correction, but made mindful of the differences in custom that are only known to a natives. I'm still glad that the Bastard family is not my direct. And I can't help but wonder if the young Bastard men had trouble attracting wives. But enough!

ROBERT GIFFORD, FIRST BARON OF ST. LEONARD'S

The youngest of all John's children was Robert, a very bright, ambitious young man whose rise was assisted by the wealth of his father and elder brothers. For years, knowing the outline of his career, I have been impressed. I still am, but now that I know more about the prejudices he faced because of the family origins in trade, I am even more impressed. Twenty-first century strivers talk about a glass ceiling. The Industrial Revolution made a 'crack,' but the English "Class System" was alive and well.

Robert Gifford was educated in Exeter by a dissenting minister, (not the traditional public school education), articled (apprenticed) with an Exeter attorney, and then moved to London where he attended Middle Temple in 1800, (akin to US Law school) and was called to the Bar in 1808. He achieved high honors in his political/legal career as he was Solicitor-General 1818 – 19; Attorney General 1819 – 24; Speaker of the House of Lords 1824 – death; Master of Rolls 1824 – death. Attorney General 1818 – 19.

As noted in The *HistoryofParliamentonline.org* he prosecuted many famous cases, and opined on many important bills. Gifford successfully conducted the Cato Street conspirators trial for the attempted assassination of the Prime Minister and his cabinet. (Some were hanged and beheaded, others transported after the original sentence of being drawn and quartered was deemed too harsh). Robert Gifford was sadly anti Irish as demonstrated by his speaking against the Catholic Relief Act in 1821. This Act, passed in the House of Commons, called on the government to cease excluding Catholics from the their civil rights purely because of their religion. Had it passed, the history of Ireland might have been very different. But, in the House of Lords it was defeated by the Peers of the realm, including our ancestor.

His next vote on an Irish question came only a year later when he supported the Catholic Insurrection Act of 1822 which forbad Irish Catholic men from leaving their homes at night. Huge numbers of English troops were stationed all over Ireland to enforce the law. They were even encouraged to inspect Catholic homes and, should a man be absent, pursue and arrest him. In an already tense Ireland, this added dramatically to the problem.

He most fascinating case, and the one for which he will be remembered is the one in which he acted on behalf of His Majesty the King, and in his role as Solicitor General, addressed the House of Lords in support of the "bill of pains and penalties against Queen Caroline; 1824".

Basically, the King accused his wife of adultery and wanted a divorce, which only Parliament could grant. But Parliament was divided by party loyalty over whether or not to grant it. The Tory party, royalists, championed King George IV who had been a great womanizer and rebel in his youth. He had secretly married his Catholic love in an Episcopal ceremony, but it was against the law for a Catholic to be Queen. Eventually, when he needed the raise in his allowance which only Parliament could give, he "forgot" this marriage and agreed to wed the German Princess, Caroline of Brunswick.

According to King George she was short, fat and ugly; she never changed her underwear, and repelled him. In spite of this and his being drunk for days, they conceived a daughter. He then told Caroline to be gone from his sight. She obliged and according to Tory sources lived in

England with lovers (never proven), dancing half-naked around the courts of Europe, settling in Italy where she behaved scandalously with an Italian lover. The Parliament demanded witnesses. Her Italian servants were the main witnesses to this behavior, and the English were not keen to hear or believe the testimony of foreigners. The case was presented for weeks, with Robert Gifford pleading for the King. He was knighted shortly thereafter.

Whig supporters and the common people disliked George IV and supported Caroline. The most notorious event in her time as Queen was the day she pounded on the doors of Westminster Abbey during her husband's coronation ceremony, demanding to be allowed in and crowned Queen. The door was slammed in her face. She died, uncrowned, a year later.

A Google search for information about Lord Gifford produced a site, *www.historyofparliamentonline.org* which had fascinating detail, some of which I will include here. Probably because of his identification with a political party, there are contradictory appraisals of Lord Gifford's skills. "His origins in Trade" were noted by one biographer, "a lawyer of good abilities, and of still better fortune whose rise to eminence from humble origins were the more remarkable as 'his powers though respectable, were not splendid, though solid not profound." A Lady Grey "reported that all the bar think him incompetent, and he himself feels it." Another said, "he has no confidence in himself, no firmness of character. He was neither at a public school, nor at a university, which is a great mis fortune to a man naturally of a timid character." *footnote 19* The old boys' club at work, or truth?

Robert Gifford had seven children with his wife, Harriet Marie Drewe who was "described as a dashing, flaunting wife, a clergyman's daughter, was said to have astonished Edinburgh society in the autumn of 1825 by her gaiety and libre conversation." In September 1926, after 'being killed by his wife' who insisted upon his traveling when unwell, he died of cholera. *Footnote 21*

But on the other hand, from members of his own party, the quotations are different. One member recalls:

an uncommon kindness of manner, an unusual sweetness of temper, a strong judgement, a vast store of professional learning." "An obituarist wrote, His leading characteristic was good sense… In the Commons…he never shone…His want of popular energy was here most apparent…as a judge, he is entitled to great praise… Cool and dispassionate, scrutinizing, patient, and impartial, he gained universal confidence…his carriage was easy, his aspect mild without any admixture of weakness. His eye was quick and intelligent; his personal manner and address calm, frank and engaging" *Footnote 23*

Who was he? A man who was surely the pride of his family, who had a reedy voice, perhaps a wild wife, certainly seven children. A Non-Conformist educated lawyer who practiced in the ranks of the Anglican, Public School and University educated men, who were never able to accept him as "one of them" despite his brilliance and perseverance. The world doesn't change very much or very easily. He was a party loyalist, who died at only 47 years old before he had achieved the next prize, the chancellorship.

Family Tree Maker tells me that he is my 1st cousin 5x removed. Lord Gifford was succeeded by his son, Robert, whose son Edric was the Third. Edric's younger brother Edgar succeeded him, and a nephew, Charles Gifford became the 5th. The present 6th Lord Gifford is Anthony, (1940 –) a barrister, educated at Cambridge, who lives and practices both in Jamaica and in London. His son, Thomas Adam is the heir apparent to the title.

EPILOGUE

The amazing 'find' of the marriage of Lewis Kelly to Charlotte Gifford in 1794 opened the door to this fascinating family line which is a genealogist's dream because of the huge resources of the National Archives of England which are not only preserved but digitized. It was fodder for an English major as I immersed myself in a culture and a history that I have loved for years. On a personal note, it brought me the wonderful friendship of Yvonne Hensman, the most brilliant researcher and patient teacher, who regularly set me on the right paths and deciphered my maddening typo-filled emails.

I hope that one day a grand or great-grand will look at this and take up the very best hobby in the world. Because it opens the world to you.

And I hope that by reading and speaking these names, your ancestors will live. To repeat the lovely quote with which I began:

'We die once when the last breath leaves our bodies. We die a second time when the last person speaks our name.' The first death is beyond our control. But the second one we can strive to prevent."

The Book of Lost Friends by Lisa Wingate 2019

APPENDICES

Appendix I

<u>**Will of John Gifford 1688**</u>

Extracted from the Registry of the Lord Bishop of Bath and Wells.

In the last Will and Testament of John Gifford late of the Parish of Wellington in the County of Somerset deceased bearing date the eighth day of June in the year of our Lord 1688 and now remaining in the Registry of the Consistorial Episcopal Court of Wells it is amongst other things therein recited as follows (to wit) "I give and devise unto Thomas Gifford my son one Close of Land commonly known by the name of Ditchford Close lying in the Parish of Wellington for terms of his natural life and after his decease to the Heirs Male of his body lawfully begotten or to be begotten and for want of such issue to my son Samuel Gifford and to the Heirs Male of his body lawfully begotten or to be begotten and for want of such issue to my son John Gifford and to the Heirs Male of his body lawfully begotten or to be begotten and for want of such issue to my Right Heirs Male for ever."

This agrees with .... Edw'd Parfitt Dop(?) Reg'r

Appendix II

Will of Thomas Gifford 1718

In the name of God Amen I Thomas Gifford of Wellington in the County of Somerset Yeoman not able in body but of sound mind and memory blessed be to God do make this my last Will and Testament refuting all former Wills in manner and form following Impris I commend my Soul to God my most merciful Father who gave it depending on the merits of my dearest Redeemer the Lord Jesus Christ Son and Eternal Salvation and my body to devout burial at the discretion of my Executrix afternamed and as for the worldly goods God hath blessed me I give and bequeath in form following Impris I give unto my beloved wife Anna Gifford all that Estate wherein I now live and the Estate adjoining called Barnwoods(?) with all appurtenances thereunto belonging during so much of the Term of Law in the said Estates as she shall happen to live provided on condition that my said wife do yield up and relinquish that Estate whereunto she is instituted by virtue of Joynture or Marriage Settlement called Dursays(?) wherein Samuel Manley my Tenant now liveth unto my son William hereafter mentioned Item I give unto my daughter Mary Buncombe a field called Ralph's......... lying within the Burrough of Wellington aforesaid immediately after my decease and I give my said daughter Mary forty pounds to be paid her in three months after my decease Item I give my son William five hundred pounds to be paid him when his Apprenticeship expireth and I give also to my said son William my Estate called Dursays(?) wherein Samuel Manley my Tenant now liveth with all my Rights and Title thereunto immediately after my decease but if it should so happen which I hope will not that my wife abovesaid will not relinquish and yield up her Right of Joynture in that Estate called Dursays(?) aforesaid then my will is that the two Estates given my wife herein about written on condition or be yielded up to my said son William within one month after my decease to whom I give the Estate I now live in and also Barnwoods(?) during so much of the term I have in the said Estates as his mother my wife abovesaid shall happen to live Also I give my said son William Ditchford Meadow immediately after my decease to him and his Heirs forever Item I give my daughter Ann five hundred pounds to be paid her in three months after my decease Item I give my son Phillip and his Heirs forever all that Estate of Land I purchased of one Bursell(?) lying in West Buckland likewise all my Right and Title to two Copyhold Tenements lying in West Buckland aforesaid called Pococks(?) Moors part of the Manor of West Buckland Likewise Pococks(?) Orchard And Fishers Land which I hold Lease lying in the parish of Aller(?) in this County which I bought of Richard Chapman I give to my son Phillip to be yielded to him immediately after my decease on this condition and proviso that my said son Phillip shall well and truly pay or cause to be paid within two years after my decease the sum of two hundred pounds to my son William abovesaid Also I give my son Phillip all my Right and Title in the Estate I live in and also Barnwoods(?) adjoining after the death of my wife abovesaid Item I give unto my daughter Sarah five hundred pounds to be paid her when she attains the age of twenty one unless she happen to marry sooner with her mother's consent and before she attains the age of twenty one or be married my will is that she be paid the sum of ten pounds yearly And my will is that if my daughter aforesaid happen to dye unmarried before she arrive at the years of twenty one aforesaid that then her portion of five hundred pounds be equally divided between the rest of my children Item I give to my brother John Gifford and to Sister Shorlands one broad peirt of gold to each of them to be paid at my decease Item I give to my sons William and Phillip aforesaid and to my daughters Mary, Ann and Sarah aforesaid to each of them I give four broad peirts of gold apiece to be paid to them within one month after my decease Item I give to my three grandchildren Mary, Joan and Ann Buncombe ten pounds apiece to be paid them as they severally arrive to the age of twenty one years Item I give to the poor of parish of Wellington three pounds to be distributed by those my Executrix hereafter named shall appoint after the rate of sixpence to a family and to the poor of West Buckland I give thirty shillings to be distributed as aforesaid sixpence to a family within one week after my burial item I give to Nicholas Gill if living in my house at my death twenty shillings Item I give to John Boyle twenty shillings when he hath served out his apprenticeship Lastly all the rest of my goods not herebefore given or bequeathed I do give and bequeath unto my beloved wife Ann Gifford aforesaid whom I appoint and ordain to be the sole Executrix of this my Will and Testament in special trust and confident that my said wife will fulfill this my last Will and Testament and see that all Debts Legacies and decent funeral expenses be discharged and that all the household goods allowing only for …. and …..be rosewood for my son Phillip aforesaid after his mother deceased In witness that this is my last Will written on two sheets of paper and sealed together I have hereunto set my hand

and seal this sixteenth day of July in the year of our Lord one thousand seven hundred and eighteen 1718 **Thomas Gifford** ./.

Signed sealed publishes and declared to be my last Will written on two sheets and sealed together in the presence of Samuel Berry John Gill the mark of John Bennett

I **Thomas Gifford** of Wellington in the County of Sommersett (sic) Yeoman have this seventeenth day of October 1718 made the underwritten Codicil to my last Will and Testament that whereas I Thomas Gifford abovesaid did in my last Will among other Gifts and Legacies given to my son William give my said son William five hundred pounds to be paid him in some short time after my decease now my said son William having already received from me four hundred pounds to be deemed and taken as part of the said Legacy and bequeathed to my said son William in witness whereof I have hereunto set my hand and seal in presence of John Gifford./.Joseph Kennaway, the mark of John Colburn, Samuel Berry./.

Appendix III

<u>**Will of Ann Norrish Gifford 2 February 1758**</u>

In the Name of God Amen

I Ann Gifford of Exeter in the County of Devon Widow at present Enjoying sound health and sound mind and memory blessed be God and man this my last will and testament first commending my soul to God who gave it in hope of Eternal happiness as through the Lord Jesus Christ and my body to devout burial awaiting for a Blessed Resurrection as for the worldly goods God has given me and I give and bequeath in manner following Imprimis I give unto Honor Gifford my Daughter-in-Law twenty pounds Item I give unto my Grandson William Gifford the Estate called Ditch..rks ? lying in the parish of Burliscombe In the County of Devon and to enter on it the next Quarter day after my decease Item I give unto my grandson John Gifford one hundred pounds Item I give unto my grandson George Gifford one hundred pounds Item I give unto my grand daughter Ann Fryer one hundred pounds Item I give unto my two Great Grandsons John and George Gifford sons of my Grandson John Gifford ten pounds each when they attain the age of twenty one years Item I give unto my Grand Daughter Mary Southwood wife of Mr. Thomas Southwood of Pitminster one hundred pounds Item I give unto Samuel Southwood Thomas Southwood and Joan Southwood Sons and daughter of Thomas Southwood and Mary Southwood ten pounds each when they shall attain the age of twenty one years Item I give unto Sarah Clermont my granddaughter at Bath one hundred pounds and such child or children she shall have at my death ten pounds each when they shall attain the age of twenty one years Then I give unto my Grand Daughter ?Honor Norman? Darman? Two hundred pounds Item I give unto my Grand daughter Mary Coad Twenty pounds when she shall attain the age of twenty one years Item I give unto my Great Grandchildren living at the time of my passing begotten on the body of my Grand Daughter Ann Flyer ten pounds each when they attain the age of twenty one years Then I give unto my Daughter in Law Agnes Gifford twenty pounds and I give unto my grandson Thomas Gifford two hundred pounds when he shall reach the age of twenty one years on account of bearing his father's name and his grand father's mourning ring Item I give unto my grand Children of my Grand Daughter Ann Bossly?)

twenty five pounds when they shall reach the age of twenty one years if one dyes before then the whole fifty pounds to the other that shall be living at the time to Mrs Bossly's Daughter if living after my death my best suit of linning and black silk gown and my .... Trunk labeled AG (or A C) Item I give to my cousin Joan Bardot two pieces of gold immediately after my decease Item I give unto my Grandson George Gifford my silver tankard Item I give one guinea to the Minister that shall preach my funeral sermon Item I give all my common wearing apparel to Elenor Shorland wife of Henry Shorland of Wallington and five shillings Unto all such Legatees as shall be of the age of twenty one years at my death my will is that they shall not demand their legacies within three months after my death Item All the rest of my goods and chattels Estates both real and personal I give to my Son Philip whom I ordain and appoint to be the whole and sole executor revoking all former wills by me made do make this to be my last will and testament he paying my Debts and funeral Expenses in witness thereof i give this my hand and seal this fourteenth day of February in the year of our lord one thousand seven hundred and fifty eight Ann Gifford

Signed and sealed published and declared by the said Ann Gifford the Testatrix as and for her last will and testament in the presence of us witnesses William Marks and Elizabeth Humet ... Peter Bardot

CODICIL May 8, 1760

Be it remembered that I Ann Gifford of Wellington in the County of Somerset widow by this as a codicil to be annexed to my last will and Testament bearing date the fourteenth day of February one thousand and fifty eight which I do hereby desire may be taken to be as fully and effectively to all intents and purposes whatsoever as part of my said Will the same as if what is hereafter mentioned was expressly given devised and bequeathed in the body of my said will in manner hereafter mentioned was expressly given devised and bequeathed in the body of my said Will in manner as hereafter mentioned whereas I have by my said Will hereto annexed given unto my Granddaughter Ann Fryer one hundred pounds and unto Mary Southwood wife of Mr. Thomas Southwood of Pitminister one hundred pounds and unto Sarah Clermont my Granddaughter of Bath one hundred pounds Now my will and meaning is and I do hereby give and bequeath the said one hundred pounds to be given by my said will as aforesaid to my said Granddaughter Ann Fryer unto my son Philip Gifford of Wellington aforesaid Gentleman his executors adminors and assigns upon this Trust hereafter mentioned and to for or upon no other Trust whatever (that is to say) upon Trust to pay the said Ann Flyer out of the interest and produce thereof the sum of four pounds a year during the term of her natural life but my will is that no interest shall be paid therefore unto Ann Flyer until three months after my demise and that the said Ann Flyer's Receipt alone notwithstanding her coverture shall from time to time during the time aforesaid a sufficient discharge to my said son of the said four pounds a year and from and after the demise of the said Ann Flyer then upon trust to pay and divide the said sum of one hundred pounds to and among all and every the children of the said Ann Flyer that shall live to attain their respective ages of twenty one years equally and share and share alike if more than one and if but one such child to such only child as soon as he she or they shall have so attained his her or their respective ages and my will is that the four pounds a year so directed to be paid as aforesaid shall from and after the death of my said granddaughter Ann Fryer be paid to and for the benefit of all and every such child and children which they shall respectively attain his or her respective age or ages aforesaid Ad Ii hereby also give and bequeath the said one hundred pounds so by my said will given and bequeathed to Mary the wife of ... Thomas Southwood as foresaid unto my said son Philip Gifford his executors and assigns upon Trust to pay the said Mary Southwood out of the interest and product thereof the sum of four pounds a year during her life and for her sole and separate use but my will is that no such interest shall be paid to her therefore until three months after my demise and that the said Mary Southwood's Receipt alone not withstanding her coverture shall be from time to time during the term aforesaid a sufficient discharge to my said Son for the said four pounds a year and from and after the demise of the said Mary then upon trust to pay and divide the said sum of one hundred pounds to and amongst all and every the children born of the said Mary Southwood that shall live to attain their respective ages of twenty one years equally and share and share alike if more than one and if but one such child or such only child as soon and he or she they shall have attained his her or their respective age or ages it is my will that the four pounds a year so divided be paid as aforesaid from and after the death of the said Mary be paid to and for the benefit of all and every child and children until they shall respectively attain such his her or their respective age of ages a aforesaid And I hereby also give and bequeath the said one hundred pounds so by my said will give to Sarah Clermont my Grand Daughter as aforesaid unto my son Philip Gifford his estate adminors and assigns upon Trust nevertheless pay the said Sarah Clermont out of the interest and product thereof the sum of four pounds a year during her life and for her sole and separate use but my will is that no such interest shall be paid to her until three months next after my demise and that the said Sarah Clermont's receipt alone not withstanding her coverture shall be from time to time during the time of a sufficient discharge to my son for the said four pounds a year and from and after the decease of the said Sarah then upon Trust to pay and divide the sum of one hundred pounds to and amongst all and every child of the said Sarah that shall have attained their respective ages of twenty one years share and share alike if more than one and if but one to such only child as soon as he she or they shall attain such his or her or their age or age last s aforesaid and my will is that the four pounds a year so directed to be paid as aforesaid shall from and after the Death of the said Sarah be paid to and for the benefit of all and every such child or children until they shall respectively attain his or her or their respective age or ages aforesaid and whereas I have not by my said will herein annexed given devised or bequeathed all that my Messuage and Tenement within the appurtenances called by the name of Broadfields and Floodgates living within the parish of West Buckland in the said County which I now hold by lease under the Bishop of Bath and Wells I do hereby give devise and bequeath with the appurt's In manner as in the other side is mentioned As to the said .Messuage and Tenement called Broadfields and Floodgates with the appurtenances I do hereby give devise and bequeath the same and every part thereof and all the Estate Tithe and Interest which I now have and which at the time of my Death I shall leave therein or thereto unto my said son Philip Gifford his sons Executors administrators and assigns in witness thereof I have to this codicils annexed to my will and testament which I again hereby desire be taken as part thereof and set my hand and seal this eighth of May in the year of our Lord one thousand seven hundred and sixty to this the last side thereof and my hand to the first side thereof ... . *Ann Gifford Ann Gifford*

Signed sealed published and declared by the testatrix Ann Gifford to the part of her last will and testament hereto annex as a Codicil thereto in the presence of us who have subscribed Our names as witnesses thereto in the presence of the said Ann Gifford and of each other .... *Robert Weston & Nash Fyne And Simon Tarra*

Appendix IV

Will of William Gifford 1753

In the Name of God Amen *I William Gifford of the City of Exon Grocer being in health of body and of sound and disposing mind and memory and understanding do make this my last Will and Testament in manner and form following first I resign my soul into the hands of God my Creator hoping to be eternally saved thro' the mediation and interfusion(?) of Jesus Christ our blessed Saviour and Redeemer and my Body I commit to the Earth to be interred at the discretion of my Executrix hereinafter named and as for and concerning my worldly Estate I give and dispose hereof in manner following that is to say I give my son William Gifford and his Heirs all my Mortgages Lands Tenements and Hereditations with the Appurtenances called Dursey's Farm Dolways and Ditchford in and on or by whatsoever name or names the same are called or known situate lying and being in the Parish of Wellington in the County of Somerset to hold the same unto and to the use of my said son William Gifford his Heirs and Assigns for ever and I further give my said son William the sum of one hundred pounds to be paid him by my Executrix within six calendar months next after my death Also I give to my son John Gifford the sum of two thousand pounds to be paid him within two calendar months next after my death or to be allotted to him out of my Stock in Trade in order to enable him to be in equal partnership therein and all the profit thereof from the time of my death until my son George Gifford's Apprenticeship shall end and expire it being my will that in the meantime my said Trade and Business shall be carried on by my dear wife and my son John Gifford for their equal benefit in proportion to the Stock that each of them shall have therein and when and as soon as my said son George's Apprenticeship shall expire I do will and direct that my said wife shall not from that time have any interest or benefit of or to any further concerns in the said Trade But that her share or part therein shall cease for the benefit of my said son George Gifford who I will and desire may from thereforth stand in the place of my said wife with respect to the said partnership and ...... therein with my said son John Gifford during their natural lives or as long as they shall mutually consent and agree so to do provided and in case my said son George Gifford do and shall pay and satisfy my said wife the full amount or value of her* *partnership Stock in the said Trade as they shall agree or otherwise as the same shall be valued between them by two indifferent persons one to be chosen on each side and in order to enable my said son George Gifford to enter into the said partnership and as a provision for him I give unto him the sum of one thousand eight hundred pounds to be paid at the expiration of his said Apprenticeship and in the meantime and until my said son George's Apprenticeship shall expire it is my will that Interest for his said Legacy shall be accounted for by my Executrix at the rate of three pounds and four shillings by the hundred by the year and a competent part thereof applied towards his maintenance and the residue thereof improved for his benefit by and at the discretion of my said Executrix But in the case my said son George shall happen to die before the end or expiration of his said Apprenticeship then and in such case I give unto William Clarke of the City of Exon Linnen Draper the sum of three hundred pounds part thereof to be paid within three calendar months next after such the death of my said son George upon Trust to be put out at Interest and as shall the Interest and produce thereof as also the said principal sum to be applied to the separate use of my daughter Ann Fryer wife of John Fryer of Merchant and her child or children or in default thereof for her Executors Administrators or Assigns in such and the same Trusts .... Intents and purposes and subject to the same provisors and Durations only as in hereinafter mentioned expressed and declared concerning the like sum of three hundred pounds hereinafter given to him the said William Clarke upon Trust as hereinafter is expressed and as to the residue of the said sum of one thousand eight hundred pounds and all the Interest and Improvement unapplied and undisposed of for the maintenance of my son George as aforesaid it is my will that the same shall go to and be equally divided amongst my said wife and the two oldest sons share and share alike Also I give unto the said William Clarke the sum of three hundred pounds to be paid to him within six calendar months next after my decease upon Trust that he the said William Clarke his Executors Administrators and Assigns do and shall from time to time lend place and keep the said sum of three hundred pounds out at Interest either or real securities or in the published Stocks or Funds at and for such Interest as he the said William Clarke his Executors Administrators and Assigns shall think fit during the natural life of the said Ann Fryer my daughter and pay and apply the Interest thereof unto my said daughter during her natural life for her separate use exclusive of her said husband and so that he shall have no power or control over the same nor shall the same be subject to his debts or Engagements and from unto after her death upon Trust to distribute and divide the said principal sum of three hundred pounds and all the Interest thereof not paid over to my said daughter unto and amongst all and every child or children of her body lawfully to be begotten in such parts shares and proportions and in such manner as my said daughter shall by any deed or writing under her hand and seal and by her executed in the presence of and attested by two or more credible witnesses or by her last Will and Testament in writing in like manner published declared and attested direct limit or appoint and in default of such Direction Limitation or Appointment to distribute and equally divide the same to and amongst all and every such child or children of my said daughter if more than one share and share alike in equal proportions one with the other and if but one then to such only child and when and as child or children shall respectively attain his several ages or marriage following that is to say to such of them as shall be a son or sons at his or their several ages of one and twenty years and to such of them as shall be a daughter or daughters as she or they shall attain her or their age or ages of one and twenty years or day of marriage which shall first happen and in the meantime to apply the Interest and Dividends thereof in and towards the maintenance and education of such child or children and in default of such Issue or in case there shall be any such and all of them shall happen to die before any one of them being a son shall attain his age of one and twenty years or any of them being a daughter shall attain her like age or marriage which shall first happen then upon Trust to pay the said sum of three hundred pounds and all the Interest and produce thereof unapplied as aforesaid or to assign and transfer the security or securities whereon the same shall be then placed unto such person or persons and in such manner as she my said daughter shall by any deed or writing or by her last Will and Testament executed and attested as aforesaid direct limit or appoint and in default of such Direction Limitations or Appointment in Trust for the Executors Administrators or Assigns of her my said daughter provided always and I do hereby declare it to be my will that it shall and may be lawful to and for the said William Clarke his Executors Administrators or Assigns by and with the consent and approbation of my said daughter testified by some writing under her hand for that purpose and not otherwise to apply all or any part of the said principal of three hundred pounds for or towards the binding or placing* out any of her child or children to such Trade Profession or Business as she shall think necessary during her lifetime or afterwards as my said Trustee shall judge proper and for their benefit and advantage and that all and every the sum or sums of money so to be paid by with and out of the said sum of three hundred pounds shall be good and effectual to all Intents and purposes against such child or children and that my said Trustee shall be indemnified and saved harmless thereinby this my will anything hereinbefore contained to the contrary thereof in any wise notwithstanding and further I do hereby will and declare that the Receipt of my said daughter alone without her said husband and notwithstanding her coverture shall be a sufficient discharge to my said Trustee for the payment of all and every the Interest Dividends and Sums of Money hereinbefore directed to be paid to her for her separate use as aforesaid and that it shall and may be lawful to and for my said Trustee his Executors Administrators and Assigns to deduct and detain by and out of the said Trust moneys and the Interest thereof all such Cost Charges Losses Damages and Expenses as he they or any of them shall sustain expend or put into in or about the Execution of the said Trusts or relating thereto and that my said Trustee his Executors Administrators or Assigns shall not be answerable or accountable for any bad or defective Security or Securities whereon the said Trust Money or any part thereof shall be at any time placed nor of any loss or losses that may happen by the altering or changing such security or securities or relating thereto or concerning the same in any sort or manner whatsoever but be always saved harmless and kept indemnified therefrom and from all damages attending the same for ever by these presents and moreover all the rest residue and remainder of all my Good Chattels Rights Credits and personal Estate of what nature or ....sooner and also the legal Estate of all forfeited Mortgages in Fee now in me vested my Debts Legacies and Funeral Expenses being first thereout paid and discharged I give and bequeath unto my dear said wife whom I make whole and sole Executrix of this my last Will and Testament hereby revoking and making void all and every former and other Will or Wills by me at any time heretofore made and Lastly it is my will and I do hereby declare that the provision hereby made for my said wife and children together with the fortune already given to my said daughter in marriage shall be and be always deemed and taken to be agreeable to my Intention and discharge of all and every sum and sums of money Estate or Estates or other provision agreed to be made to and for them any or either of them by the Articles entered into by me upon my marriage with my said wife or by any other Articles Covenant or engagement at any time entered into by me or any Demand whatsoever by them or either of them upon or against my Estate for any matter cause or thing whatsoever in witness whereof I have hereunto set my hand and seal and publishes and declared the same to be my last Will and Testament this eighth day of January in the year of our Lord one thousand seven hundred and fifty three. **William Gifford**

Signed sealed published and declared by the said testator William Gifford as and for his last Will and Testament in the presence of us three who have set our names as witnesses thereto in the presence of the said Testator and of each other and at his request. John Berry, Benjamin Withers, Jn'n Sandford

Whereas I **William Gifford** have by my above Will dated the eighth day of January one thousand seven hundred and fifty three given to my son John Gifford the sum of two thousand pounds and made such other provisions for him as are therein expressed and whereas my said son John Gifford hath lately with my consent inter married Mrs Anna Lee on which marriage I gave and obliged myself to pay and settle upon him two thousand five hundred pounds and also this house I live in after my death as a provision for him and which I intended and designed to be an equivalent and satisfaction for the said Legacy and other provision given to and made for him by my said Will and therefore I do by this my Codicil wrote underneath my said Will and which I demand shall be always esteemed and taken to be part thereof revoke the said Legacy and provision expressed or mentioned to be given or made for my said son John in and by my said Will. But I do hereby ratify and confirm my said Will in all other respects not revoked or altered by this my Codicil in witness whereof I have hereunto set my hand and seal this twenty fifth day of December one thousand seven hundred and fifty three. **William Gifford** Signed sealed published and declared by the abovenamed William Gifford as and for a Codicil to be annexed to his last Will and Testament in the presence of us who have hereunto subscribed our name John Ley

Jn'n Sandford

This Will was proved at London with a Codicil the seventh day of February in the year of our Lord One thousand seven hundred and fifty eight before the Right and Honorable Sir George Lee Knight Doctor of Laws Master Keeper or Commisary of the prerogative Court of Canterbury lawfully constituted by the Oath of Honour Gifford Widow the Relict of the deceased and sole Executrix named in the said Will to whom Administration was granted of all and singular the Goods Chattels and Credits of the said deceased this having been first sworn by Commission duly to administer.

Transcribed by Yvonne Hensman
February 2016

Appendix V

<u>Will of Honour Hutchings Gifford 1760</u>

I Honour Gifford of the city of Exon Widow do make and appoint this writing to be and remain my last will and testament in manner and form following (that is to say) first I give and bequeath to my son John Gifford the sum of three hundred pounds to be paid him within six months next after my death for his own use and Benefit and I also give to my son John the sum of sixty pounds on Trust to be equally divided between his three sons John, George, and William. Also I give to my sons William and John the sum of six hundred pounds on Trust to be placed at Interest at the end of six months next after my death on real Security or Securities or in the public stocks and to pay and apply the Interest or produce thereof unto my daughter Ann Fryer the wife of John Fryer of Oporto, Merchant during the joint lives of my said Daughter and her said husband for her separate use and Benefit exclusive of her said husband and so as that he may not have any power over the same and I do direct and appoint that the Receipt or appointment of my said Daughter only under her hand attested from time to time by one credible witness shall her good and sufficient discharge for said interest money on Trust also that if my said Daughter outlives her said husband to pay the said Principal sum of six hundred pounds and all the Interest then in arrear thereon if any or to transfer the securities subsisting for the same at the time of the death of her husband unto my said Daughter for her own use and benefit and also on this further Trust if my daughter shall fortune to die in the lifetime of her said husband and shall leave any child or children at the time of her death in that case to distribute and divide the said principal of six hundred pounds and all the interest if any then in arrear thereon and all the Interest that may then after grew out thereon amongst the children of my said Daughter if more than one when and as such children shall come to the age of twenty-one years in such shares and proportions as my said Daughter by any Deed or writing under her hand and seal attested by two or more credible witnesses or by her last will Testament in writing or by any writing purporting her last will and testament to be located and attested as aforesaid shall Direct and appoint and in default of such Direction or Appointment to Distribute and Divide the said principal sum of six hundred pounds and also the interest so in arrear and to grow out thereon from the death of my said Daughter unto and among the children of my said Daughter when and or the children of my said Daughter [two lines of erasures] shall come to the age of twenty one years equally between them and if there shall be no but one such child of my Daughter or if more than one and only one shall live to the age of twenty one years in that case to pay the whole of the said Principal sum and such Interest as aforesaid to that one or only child when such one or only child shall attain the said age of twenty one years and in the mean time to improve and stimulate the Interest as often as it shall come to a competent sum of money in like manner and for the same use and purposes as the principal is to be improved by virtue of these articles and also on this further Trust that if my said Daughter shall not leave any child or children at the time of her death or if she shall leave any and such child and if any or all such children if more than one shall fortune to die whilst under the age of twenty one years In that case, my son William my Executor herein after named shall retain one half of the Trust money so given by this article and of the interest in arrear thereon at the time of the death of my said Daughter, and to grow out and be Improved thereon from that time, to the only use and Benefit of my said son William and shall pay the other half part of such principal and Interest to my son George for his use and Benefit and I give to my said Daughter Fryer all my best wearing Apparel and my Gold watch and my best Diamond Ring and my Silver Waiter (?) marked AGHG May 21 1737 and a Silver Tankard [erasures] and my will further is that it shall and may be lawful to and for my said Sons William Gifford and John Gifford and the survivor of them his Executors and Administrators to deduct and retain from and out of the said Trust sum of six hundred pounds so given by this Article and from the Interest thereof all such costs charges losses Damages and Expenses as they or either of them shall expend sustain or be put into the Execution of the Trust reposed in them by this Article and that the said William Gifford and John Gifford or either of them or the Executors or Administrators of the survivor of them shall not be answerable or accountable for any bad or defective security or securities that shall happen to be taken for the said sum of six hundred pounds or the interest thereof or any part thereof nor for any loss or Losses that may happen therein or thereby or by changing or altering any such security or securities or relating thereto, with alteration they are at liberty to make as often as it shall seem necessary And that they the said William Gifford and John Gifford shall not be answerable and accountable for the Arts or receipts the one or the other of them but each of them for his own Arts and Receipts only Also I give to my son George the sum of seven hundred pounds to be paid him at the end of three months next after my death And whereas my dear husband did by his Last Will and Testament Declare his Will to be that from the time of his Death until the Apprenticeship of the said George Gifford our son should expire my said husband's Trade and Business should be carried on by me and by our son John and that when as soon as our said Son George's apprenticeship should expire I should not from that time be any further concerned in the said Trade and that my share therein should cease for the Benefit of our son George who was from thenceforth to stand in my place with respect to the said partnership Now in as much as my said son George hath not been concerned in the said Partnership Trade, Therefore to avoid all Disputes relating thereto I do by this my Will Direct and appoint that my said son George shall not be entitled to receive the said legacy of seven hundred pounds so by me being to him given by this my will until he doth by writing under his hand attested by one credible Witness and left with his said Brother William my Executor make all claim and Demands on my share or part of the said Partnership Trade by virtue of the Directions contained in the said Will for his standing in my place with respect to the said partnership or relating thereto. Also I give to my son John the counters shelves and .... and to my son George the .... Scales and Weights used in our Partnership Trade. Also I give to my Brother Thomas Hutchings the annual or yearly sum of five pounds to be paid to him at the end of every year that he shall happen to live next after my death by my Executor the first five pounds to be paid at the end of every year next after my death and so to be continued from year to year during his life and no longer. Also I give to each of my three sisters .... Southings Margaret Bowring and Jane Southings the sum of ten pounds and I give my ordinary or common Wearing apparel to my said three sisters equally between them. And my will is that my daughter in law Mrs. Gifford shall be the Judge to determine what shall be deemed to be my best wearing apparel and what shall be deemed my common or ordinary wearing apparel and I give to Elizabeth Bunt my late servant the sum of ten pounds and lastly all my share and interest in partnership stock and Trade and all the residue and remainder of my Goods chattels Estate and Effects of what nature or kind soever either in my own Right or as residuary legatee and executrix of my late Husband I give and bequeath unto my said on William and do make my son William whole and sole Executor of this my Last Will and Testament and so revoke all Wills by me heretofore made in witness whereof I the said

Honour Gifford have to this my last will and Testament contained in four sheets of paper set my hand and seal (that is to say) my hand to the first three sheets and my hand and seal to this last sheet this fifth day of January in the thirty third year of the Reign of his Majesty King George the second over Great Britain and in the year of Our Lord one thousand seven hundred and sixty **Honour Gifford** *This writing contained in four sheets of paper was signed by Mrs. Honour Gifford the Testatrix on the first three sheets and by her sign'd and seal'd on this last sheet and by her published and declared to be and contain her last Will and Testament in the presence of us after the Interlineation of these words "either in my own Right or as residuary Legatee and Executrix of my said deceased husband"*

Benj Withers Will Williams Theo Sweeting

THIS WILL was roved at London eighth day of February in the year of our Lord one thousand seven hundred and sixty before the Right Worshipfull Edward Simpson Doctor of Laws Master Keeper or Commissioner of the prerogative court of Canterbury lawfully constituted by the oath of William Gifford Doctor of Physick the son of the deceased and sole Executor named in the said will to whom Administration was granted of all and singular the goods chattels and credits of the said deceased having been first sworn by commission duly to administer,

Appendix VI

Will of William Gifford 1788

In the name of God Amen *I William Gifford of the City of Exeter Doctor of Physick do make and ordain this my last Will and Testament as follows Firstly I give and bequeath unto my natural or reputed son commonly called or known by the name of Henry Gifford the sum of four hundred and sixty pounds to be paid to him within three months next after my death but in case an ensign's Commission in the Army should be purchased for him before my death (which is intended to be done) then this Legacy shall be absolutely null and void. Also I give and bequeath the sum of four hundred pounds nominal stock in the three percent consolidated annuities unto Thomas Gifford of Ford in the county of Somerset, Gentleman, George Gifford of the City of Exeter, Gentleman, and John Bowring of the Parish of Saint Leonard's in the county of Devon, Fuller, on Trust for my natural or reputed son commonly called or known by the name of Samuel Gifford until he shall attain the age of twenty one years and if he shall live to attain that age then upon Trust that they my said Trustees or the survivor or survivors of them or the Executors or Administrators of such survivor do and shall pay or transfer the said sum of four hundred pounds stock unto him the said Samuel Gifford on his attaining that age for his own use and benefit and I also give and bequeath the further sum of five hundred pounds nominal stock in the three percent consolidated annuities unto the said Thomas Gifford George Gifford and John Bowring on trust for my natural or reputed daughter commonly called or known by the mane of Matilda Gifford until she shall attain her age of twenty one years and if she shall live to attain that age then upon Trust that they my said Trustees or the survivor or survivors of them or the Executors or Administrators do and shall pay the said sum of five hundred pounds stock unto her the said Matilda Gifford on her attaining that age for her own use and benefit and I also give and bequeath on her the further sum oh five hundred pounds nominal stock in the three percent consolidated annuities unto the said Thomas Gifford George Gifford and John Bowring on Trust for my natural or reputed daughter commonly called or known by the name of Charlotte Gifford until she shall attain her age of twenty one years and if she shall live to attain that age then upon trust that they my said Trustees or the survivor or survivors of them or the Executors or Administrators do and shall* *pay unto her the said Charlotte Gifford on her attaining that age for her own use and benefit but in case the said Samuel Gifford Matilda Gifford or Charlotte Gifford or any or either of them shall happen to die under the age of twenty one years then such sum of money or stock so given in Trust for such deceased child or children shall upon Trust by my said Trustees unto the surviving children on their attaining the age of twenty one years and the said Henry Gifford if he shall be then living equally to be divided and parted between them share and share alike But in the case all such children but one shall happen to die under the age of twenty one years then such sums or sums of money or stock so before given in Trust for such deceased children shall upon Trust for and paid or transferred by my said Trustees unto such only surviving child on his or her attaining the age of twenty one years and the said Henry Gifford if then living equally to be divided between them share and share alike for his or their own use and benefit if all such children happen to die under the age of twenty one years living … before …the said Henry Gifford then I give all such sums of money or stock unto him for his own use and benefit and I hereby order and direct that the Interest Dividends and produce of the said several sums of money ot stock or a competent part thereof shall be applied by my said Trustees or the survivors or survivor of them his Executors and Administrators in and towards the maintenance and education of my said children until they attain their respective ages of twenty one years Also I hereby give and devise one undivided fourth part of and in all Messuages and Tenements and Hereditaments and real Estate whatsoever and wheresoever unto and to the use of my said natural or reputed son commonly called or known as Henry Gifford and his Heirs and Assigns for ever and I hereby give and devise the remaining three fourth parts of and in my said Messuages Lands Tenements and Hereditaments and real estate whatsoever and wheresoever unto the said Thomas Gifford George Gifford and John Bowring their Heirs and Assigns to the use of them their Heirs and Assigns on Trust to pay and apply the rents and Profits thereof or a competent part thereof in and towards the maintenance and education of my other natural or reputed children commonly called or known by the names of Samuel Gifford Matilda Gifford and Charlotte Gifford equally amongst them until they shall severally reach the age of twenty one years or die which shall first happen and if they shall all live to attain that age respectively Then I give and devise the said three fourth parts of and in my said Lands Tenements and Hereditaments unto the said Samuel Gifford Matilda Gifford and Charlotte Gifford and their several heirs and Assigns for ever as Tenants in common and not as joint Tenants and if any or either of them the said Samuel Gifford Matilda Gifford and Charlotte Gifford shall happen to die under the age of twenty one years Then I give and devise the share and shares of such of them so dying of and in the said three fourth Parts of my Lands Tenements and Hereditaments unto the survivors or survivor of them if more than one living to that age and the said Henry Gifford if then living and his Heirs and Assigns for ever as Tenants in Common not as joint Tenants and if there shall be but one survivor Then to such one and the said Henry Gifford if then living and their several heirs and Assigns for ever as Tenants in Common and not as joint Tenants. But if all such children shall happen to die under the age of twenty one years leaving the said Henry Gifford Then I give and devise all my Lands Tenements and Hereditaments unto the said Henry Gifford his Heirs and Assigns for ever and I hereby authorize and empower my said Trustees and the survivors or survivor of them and the Heirs Executors and Administrators of such survivors to grant my Lease or Leases from time to time during the Minority of my said children of all or any of my Messuages Lands Tenements and Hereditaments at yearly Back rents but none of such leases shall exceed the term of seven years provided always and I hereby authorize and empower the said Thomas Gifford George Gifford and John Bowring and the survivors or survivor of them and their Heirs Executors and Administrators f such survivor if they shall think fit by and with the consent approbation and concurrence of the said Henty Gifford at anytime or times after my death absolutely to sell and dispose of my Dwelling house and appurtenances in Friernhay Lane in the said City of Exeter wherein I now live and grant and convey the same unto and to the use of any purchaser or purchasers his her or their Heirs and Assigns for ever as t the money thereby arising on Trust that they my said Trustees and survivors and survivor of them and the Executors and Administrators of such survivor do and shall make an equal division thereof into four parts and pay and apply one fourth part thereof unto the said Henry Gifford his executors Administrators and Assigns for his or their own benefit and disposal and the three remaining fourth parts shall be upon Trust for my said other children Samuel Gifford Matilda Gifford and Charlotte Gifford equally between them in the same manner on the same Trust and with the like benefit of survivorship as in herebefore mentioned and declared with regard to the several sums of money or stock in the three percent Annuities in the former part of this my Will. Also all the rest and residue of my Goods Chattels*

Rights Credits Mortgages in Fee and for Term of years ready money and securities for money personal and testamentary Estate and Effects whatsoever and wheresoever after payment of my Debts Legacies and funeral Charges I hereby give and bequeath unto Martha Whitelock sole Executrix of this my last Will and Testament Lastly my will and meaning is and I hereby order and direct that my said Trustees shall not be answerable or accountable the one for the other of them nor for the Acts Deeds Receipts and Payments only and that they shall not be charged or chargeable with or accountable for any Loss or Losses that may happen to arise in the execution of the said Trust so as the same be occasioned by or by their or either of their willful default or neglect and that they shall and lawfully may alter and change my Security or Securities and call I and place out the money due upon thereon when and as often as they think proper and that they shall and lawfully may deduct detain and allow unto themselves respectively out of my Trust Estate or some part thereof all such Costs Losses Damages Charges and Expenses whatsoever as they or any or either of them shall may reasonably or necessarily bear sustain or be put to I and about the Execution of the said Trustor anything relating thereto in Witness whereof I the said William Gifford the Testator have to the first and second sheets of this my last Will and Testament contained in three sheets of paper subscribed my name and to the third and last sheet thereof set my hand and sea this twenty sixth day of October in the year of our Lord One thousand seven Hendren and eighty seven **William Gifford**

Signed sealed published and declared by the said William Gifford the Testator as and for his last Will and Testament in the presence of us who at the request and in the sight and presence of the said Testator and of each other have subscribed our names as witnesses thereto after the interlineation in the first sheet of the words "Parish of St Leonard's in the County of Devon" A Phillips Henry Smith William Fryer jun'r

14 November 1788 The above Will was duly proved in the Prerogative Court of the Archbishop of Canterbury by the said Martha Whitelock sole Executrix thereof.

Transcribed by Yvonne Hensman, February 2016
Retyped by Nancy Ronning, February 2020

Appendix VII

<u>*Will of Martha Whitelock 1798*</u>

In the name of God amen. *I Martha Whitelock of Exeter, Spinster, do make and ordain this my last Will and Testament as follows First I give to my Niece Mary Whitelock ten Guineas to Harriet Gifford, daughter of John Gifford of Exeter Linen Draper ten Guineas to George Gifford of the same place, Gentleman And John Bowring of the Parish of Saint Leonard's in the county of Devon Fuller (my executors in trust hereinafter appointed) twenty Guineas each and it is my Will that these Legacies be paid within six months next after my death.*

Also whereas I and .my natural daughter Matilda now wife of John Hucks of Leeds In the County of York Esquire, some time before her marriage entered into and executed A bond unto Barings, Short and Cole of Exeter Merchants and partners, whereby we jointly and severally Grant into them for the payment of four hundred pounds with lawful Interest on a day therein mentioned which the Bond Was intended to secure money afterwards advanced by them to my natural son Samuel Gifford of the City of Exeter Dyer. Now it is my will and I hereby direct that it is the said John Hucks shall Hereafter be called on to pay the whole or any part of the money secured By the said Bond that then he shall be indemnified and reimbursed out of my Residuary Estate by my said Trustees and Executors In trust for whatever money he may be so obliged to pay in consequence of the said Bond Also whereas I am entitled to the sum of one hundred pounds and interest by virtue of Mortgage dated the Fourth day of February one thousand seven hundred thirty on a third part of a Capital Messuage with the Appurts called Ford and of two little Closes called the Oakhays and of our Meadow called Ford Meadow and of our other Meadow called Durlesmoor situate In the parish of Morton Hampstead In Devon for the Residue of a term of one thousand years Now I hereby give the said mortgage and all my interest therein together with all the money that shall be one thousand for Principal and Interest at the time of my death unto the said George Gifford and John Bowring their Executors and Assigns upon trust to pay and apply to the interest thereof from time to time into the hands of the said Matilda Hucks for her own sole and separate use comfort and disposal whatever exclusive of her present or any future husband, and so as the same shall not be subject or liable to his Control Debts or Engagements for and during so many years as she shall happen to live and her ... alone Shall be sufficient discharges to my said trustees and from and immediately after her death upon Trust for all and every child or children of her the said Martha Hucks that shall be then living in such parts shares and proportions, manner and form as she the said Matilda Hucks whether married or sole by her last Will and Testament in writing or any writing purporting to be such by her signed sealed and published in the presence of and attested to by two or more credible witnesses shall give short Limit or appoint and for want thereof upon Trust for such child or all such children (if there shall be more than one) of her the said Matilda Hucks that shall be living at the time of her death equally to be divided and parted between them share and share alike for his or her or their own use and benefit but if there shall be no such child or children then living then upon Trust for such person or persons in such parts shares and proportions manner and form as she the said Matilda Hucks by her last will and testament executed and attested as aforesaid shall give short limits or appoint and for want thereof use upon Trust for the Executors or trustees of the said Matilda Hucks Also all the rest and residue of my goods, chattel, rights Credits Stock in the public funds monies and securities for money and personal Estate and Effects of what nature or kind soever subject in the first place to the payment of my debts the aforesaid Legacies And my funeral expenses I hereby give and bequeath unto the said George Gifford and John Bowring their executors and Trustees upon trust for my three natural children the said Samuel Gifford Matilda Hucks and Charlotte now the wife of Lewis Kelly lately Cornet in the Twelfth Regiment of Eight Dragoons in the manner Following (that as to say) as to one third part of my Residuary Estate and Effects the whole in these parts to be equally divided upon trust for the said my son Samuel Gifford and to be applied laid out and disposed of for his benefit by my said Trustees in such a way and manner as they of the survivor of them his Executor or trustees shall think fit and I leave it to their discretion either to pay him the Interest only or the whole, or such part of the principal as they think proper and as to our other their third part of my said Residuary Estate upon Trust that the said George Gifford and John Bowring or the survivor of them his Executors or trustees shall put place and hand out or continue the same at Interest or such security or securities as they shall think fit and interest on such Government or Real or private and personal Securities as they shall think fit and the interest thereof as well as the Principal sum or Sums shall be for the benefit of the same Matilda Hucks on the same Trust trusts and to and for the same.in the ….. and purposes as are hereintofore particularly mentioned expressed and declared ofa nd concerning the … sum of one hundred pounds and interest in the said Mortgage and as to the remaining third of my said Residuary Estate and Effects upon Trust that the said George Gifford and John Bowring or the survivor of then his executors and trustees do and .shall put place and hand out or continue the same at Interest or with Government or Real or private and personal security or securities As they shall think fit and pay and apply the Interest Dividends and profit thereof from time to time into the hands of the said Charlotte Kelly for her own sole and separate use benefit and disposal exclusive of her present or any future husband and so as the same shall not be subject or liable to his Control Debts or Engagements for and during so many years as she shall happen to live and her receipts and … shall be sufficient I hereby charge to my said trustees and from and immediately after her death upon Trust for all and every child or children of the said Charlotte Kelly that shall be living at the time of her death in such parts shares and proportions in manner and form as she the said Charlotte Kelly whether married or sole by her last Will and Testament in writing or any writing purported to be such to be by her duly signed sealed and published in the presence of and attested to by two or more credible witnesses shall give or appoint and for want thereof upon trust for all such child or children if there shall be more than one of her the said Charlotte Kelly that shall be living at the time of her death equally to be divided and parted between them share and share alike for … her or their use and benefit but if there shall be no child or children then living then upon trust for such person or persons and in such parts shares and proportions manner and form as she the said Charlotte Kelly by such her last will and testament executed and attested as aforesaid shall give …. or appoint and for want thereof upon Trust for such child or all such children (if there shall be more than one) of her the late Charlotte Kelly that shall be living at the time of her death equally to be divided and parted between them share and share alike for his her or their own use and benefit but if there shall be no such child or children then living then upon Trust for such son or persons and in such part shares and proportions manner and form as she the said Charlotte Kelly by such her last Will and Testament executed and attested as aforesaid shall give short limit or appoint and for want thereof upon Trust for the Executor or Administrators of her the said Charlotte Kelly Also I hereby nominate and appoint the said George

THE GIFFORDS OF EXETER

Gifford and John Bowring Executors in Trust of this my last will and testament, Lastly it is my will and meaning that my said Trustees and Executors in Trust shall not be answerable or accountable the one for the other of them nor for the other of them nor the one for the others debts but each for himself and for his own debts Receipts and Payments only and that it shall be lawful for them or the survivor of them his Executors or Trustees to sell and convert into money such parts of my Effects as they shall think fit and that they shall and may from time to time call in and place out the said Trust Monies and alter and change the Security or Securities on which the same may be but when And as often as they shall judge it expedient and shall not be answerable of any bad or insufficient Security or bad Securities and that they shall lawfully ... reimburse himself or themselves out of the said Trust Estate all such Costs Charges and Expenses whatsoever as shall be incurred or occasioned by the said Trust or anything relative thereto or witness whereof I the said Martha Whitelock the Testatrix have here unto set my hand and seal this sixteenth day of February in the year of our Lord one thousand seven hundred and ninety five **Martha Whitelock**

Signed sealed published and delivered by the said Martha Whitelock Testatrix as and for her last will and testament in the presence of us Ro**bert Gifford Wearman Gifford**

Codicil to be ... and taken as part of my last Will and Testament on the other side I hereby give to Dorothy Gifford wife of Mr John Gifford of Exon senior? Linen Draper ten Guineas as a mark of my regard for her and it is my will that this Legacy be paid at the same time as the other Legacies given by my said will And I confirm my said will in all other respects In witness thereof I have to this codicil set my hand and seal this eighteenth day of February one thousand seven hundred ninety five By the said Martha Whitelock signed sealed and published and delivered by the said Martha Whitelock as and for a Codicil to her last Will and Testament in the presence of us **Robert Gifford Wearman Gifford**

This will was proofed in London with a codicil the 18th day of April 1798 before the Right Honorable Sir Williiam....etc.

Appendix VIII

<u>Will of Charlotte Gifford – 1849</u>

This is the last Will and testament of me Charlotte Kelly the wife of Lewis Kelly of Kildare in the County of Kildare Esquire whereas in and by the settlement made previous to my marriage dated the ninth day of January one thousand seven hundred and ninety four a power is reserved to and vested in me of giving and bequeathing the lands and money thereon settled and in - the lands should be sold then of giving and appointing the money arising from the sale thereof after the death of my said husband to and amongst the children of the said marriage and if there should be none then to any other person or persons at my discretion by deed or will executed in the presence of three credible witnesses And whereas in and by the will of my mother deceased dated the eighteenth day of February one thousand seven hundred and ninety five the Rite power is reserved to and vested in me of giving and appointing the money and properties thereby given and bequeathed in the same manner as by the said marriage settlement And whereas the lands comprised in and conveyed by the said marriage settlement have been long since sold and the money arising from the sale thereof has been placed in the funds in the names of George Gifford of the City of Exeter Esquire and of John Bowring of Exeter Merchant And whereas there is now belonging to me under and by virtue of the said marriage settlement and will of my said late mother the several sums of one thousand eight hundred and twelve pounds seven shillings and three pence now vested in the now three and a half per cents and four hundred pounds - and also three hundred and three pounds fifteen shillings Bank Stock and four hundred pounds... to John Hucks of Foxdown in the parish of Parkham in the County of Devon Esquire - In trust for the use and purposes therein aforementioned that is to say I give and bequeath unto my six daughters Catherine Kelly Charlotte Kelly Eliza Kelly Mary Kelly Matilda Kelly and Anne Kelly the sum of one thousand eight hundred and twelve pounds seven shillings and three pence now three and a half per cents and the sum of three hundred and three pounds fifteen shillings Bank Stock to be divided equally between them and to be paid them on the day of marriage or when the youngest should attain the age of twenty one years and if any of my said daughters should die before the youngest has attained the age of twenty one years then their share to be equally divided between the surviving sisters And I do thereby give and bequeath the sum of four hundred pounds - after deducting the money necessary to defray my funeral expenses in the following manner I give and bequeath unto my son Thomas he being already provided for by his Grandfathers will the sum of five guineas for a ring as a token of my maternal regard and the remainder to be equally divided between my three sons Lewis Kelly William Kelly and Henry Kelly to be paid them as they respectively attain the age of twenty one years and do hereby nominate and appoint the said John Huckes of Foxdown aforesaid to be sole Executor of this my will and witnessed - - - my hand and seal this eleventh day of February one thousand eight hundred and thirty three. Charlotte Kelly Signed sealed published and declared by the said Charlotte Kelly as and for her last Will and testament in the presence of us who in her presence and the presence of each other have scribed our names as witnesses there --- Robert Roberts – Evan Roberts – William Roberts

....

On the 19th August 1845 ano domini with the will annexed of the goods chattles and credits of Charlotte Kelly wife of Lewis Kelly heretofore Gifford late of Aber in the County of Carnarvon deceased limited only so far as a remaining sum of four hundred pounds three per cent annuities and one undivided fourth part of and in the real estate of William Gifford late of the City of Exeter Doctor of Physic deceased or the money which may have arisen by the sale thereof or the stock funds and annuities whereon the same may now be invested and the interest divided as procurements and profits thereof which since the death of the said Lewis Kelly have become one and are now unapplied and also one third party or share of the residuary estate of Martha Whitelock late of the City of Exeter Spinster deceased and all savings and accumulations which she the said Charlotte Kelly deceased may have made from her said separate estate and property which by virtue of a certain Bond or Obligation becoming date the ninth day of January in the year one thousand seven hundred and ninety four and the will of the said Martha Whitelock deceased she had a right to dispose of and appointed accordingly but no further or otherwise in any other manner whatsoever was granted to Mary Kelly Spinster the daughter of the said deceased and one of the principal legatees named in the said will She having been first sworn by common duty to administer John Hucks the sole Executor named in the said will having died without having taken upon himself the Probate and execution thereof and Anne Kelly wife of Waldron Kelly a principal legatee also named in the said will the youngest daughter of the said Charlotte Kelly deceased - - attaining the age of twenty one years.

Transcript of Memorials of Deeds and Wills
1840 Volume 15 # 189 LDS FILM # 0548215

Kelly and Kelly
Marriage Settlement
____27ᵗʰ Day on July
_____ Between 3 & 4 o'clock

To the Register appointed by Act of Parliament for registering Deeds Wills and so forth in Ireland.

A Memorial of an Indented deed of Settlement bearing date the twenty first day of July one thousand eight hundred and forty and made between Waldron Kelly of Lower Rutland Street in the City of Dublin, Gentleman of the first part Anne Kelly fifth daughter of Lewis Kelly of the town of Kildare, Esquire and now wife of the said Waldron Kelly of the second part and James Terence Duggan of Richmond Street in said City of Dublin doctor of Medicine and Marmaduke Bell of Kilcullen in said county of Kildare, Doctor of Medicine of the third part reciting that a marriage had lately been solemnized between said Waldron Kelly and Ann Kelly and that said Waldron Kelly was seized and posesed (?) of the land and premises herein after mentioned said indenture witnessed that the said Waldron Kelly did for the consideration herein mentioned grant bargain sell and release and confirm unto the said James Terrance Duggan and Marmaduke Bell in their actual posesion (?) then being be virtue of the deed and statute therein recited and to their heirs and assigns All that those the lands of the White Abbey near the Town of Kildare and all that those premises and near the Town of Kildare held under the Dean and Chapter of Kildare and all that and those the Lodge Stables and lands adjoining the Curragh of Kildare held index Nicholas Ormsby Esquire and his Estate right title and interest of ire(?) to or cut of the said lands tenants and premises To hold for the several terms for which said land and premises are respectively held upon Trust to the use of the said Waldron Kelly for life until he should fail in his credit or become Insolent or Bankrupt then to the use of the said Anne Kelly for life free from control or intermeddling of the said Waldron Kelly and from his debts liabilities or engagements notwithstanding coverture and upon the other trusts therein mentioned and after further reciting as therein said Indenture further witnessed , that the said Waldron Kelly and Anne Kelly *according to several and respective rights did grant th___ ___ sell assign transfer and make over unto the said James Terence Duggan and Marmaduke Bell All that and those the one fifth part or proportion of the sum of one thousand eight hundred and twelve pounds seven shillings and three pence new three and a half percent Stock and three hundred and three pounds sixteen shillings Bank Stock therein mentioned to which one fifth the said same Kelly would on the death of her father the said Lewis Kelly become _____ under the provisions of the Will of her Mother the late Mrs. Charlotte Kelly upon trust to lay out the same in a purchase of houses or lands or otherwise invest the same as the said Anne Kelly and Waldron Kelly should approve of and pay the annual produce thereof to the said Waldron Kelly for life until he should fail in his credit or become Insolvent or Bankrupt then upon Trust to the said Anne Kelly for life free from control or intermeddling of her said husband and freed from his debts liabilities or engagements notwithstanding her coverture and upon the further trusts in said deed mentioned which said Deed and this Memorial are respectively witnessed by Edmond Mooney of the City of Dublin Gentleman and Peter McNally of same Place writing Clerk Waldron Kelly (Seal) Signed and Sealed in presence of Edmond Mooney Peter McNally = The above named Edmond Mooney make oath and saith he is a subscribing Witness to the Deed of which the above writing is a Memorial and to the above Memorial saith he saw said deed executed by the said Waldron Kelly Anne Kelly and James Terrence Duggan and the said Memorial by the said Waldron Kelly Saith the name Edmond Mooney subscribed to said Deed and Memorial as a Witness thereto in this Deponints(?) proper name other divesting Saith that on Monday the twenty fourth day of July one thousand eight-hundred and forty he Deponent delivered said deed and Memorial to Walter Glascock Esquire assistant Register at the Registry Office at the Kings Inn City of Dublin between the hours of three and four o'clock in the afternoon for the purpose of having same duly registered Edmond Mooney = Sworn before me this 27th day of July 1840*

Walter Glascock AR Eleven sheets
A true Copy R Rogers

ABOUT THE AUTHOR

Nancy O'Connell Ronning is a retired librarian who holds an MS in LS, the Master's Degree in Library Service from Columbia University, and an MS in Literature and Education from Hunter College of the City of New York. She served as a reference librarian in universities and business, and spent many years as a High School Librarian.

She began to learn genealogical skills with courses at the New York Genealogical and Biographical Society; was a Fellow at the National Institute for Genealogical Research in Washington, DC; and continues her education at seminars and with membership in the Genealogical Society of Bergen County and the Monmouth County Genealogical Society.

Research trips to Ireland and England, and traveling to the home towns and cities of all but one of her great-grandparents has given her a depth of feeling for, and a broader appreciation of their lives. It has enabled her to know them in some small way.

Previous books are *The Kellys of Kildare The Story of an Irish Family Line through Three Hundred Years, Volume I: The Story.* LinDoc Press, 2014. *The Kellys of Kildare The Story of an Irish Family Line through Three Hundred Years, Volume II: The Sourcebook.* LinDoc Press, 2014. LinDocPress@gmail.com

She lives in Marlboro, New Jersey, has two daughters and four grandchildren. nronning@yahoo.com